# FROM
# VISION
## TO
# IMPACT

## THE SECRETS TO BUILDING A SUCCESSFUL SOCIAL ENTERPRISE

EARL MARTIN PHALEN

Published in Bridgeport, CT by Faithwork Press, a trademark of Faithwork Production, LLC.

ISBN: 978-1-964018-00-3 (Paperback edition)

ISBN: 978-1-964018-01-0 (eBook edition)

Library of Congress Control Number:

www.faithworkproduction.com

# Dedication

*Dedicated to mom and dad, Veronica and George Phalen, my siblings and all of the teachers, coaches, mentors and friends who shaped my life and leadership.*

# Foreword

There is no more important obligation the citizens in a democratic society have to the children and youth than to provide them with opportunities to develop their talent. The legitimacy of that democracy rests on those opportunities. When those opportunities are real and available, students can develop the skills to improve their lives and to contribute to improving their communities. When those opportunities are lacking, cycles of poverty and disadvantage are perpetuated, people lose faith in themselves and in society, and communities and societies decline. As they do, people lose faith in democracy and in a social contract that has failed to include them.

Sustaining a vibrant democracy therefore rests on sustaining effective educational institutions. Doing this requires entrepreneurial leadership, the leadership to create the necessary innovations so schools can successfully educate all children well. This book is essential reading for those entrepreneurial leaders.

In clear and engaging prose *From Vision to Impact: The Secrets to Building a Successful Social Enterprise* walks the reader through all the key steps of creating and sustaining an effective educational and social enterprise. The book lays out seven building blocks of social entrepreneurial ventures: developing clear purpose, building the right team, articulating a business plan, developing a financial engine, leading to prioritize problem solving, building a culture that empowers the team, and maintaining faith and managing one's emotions in service of the children and youth we seek to serve.

The author, Earl Martin Phalen, writes based on a deep, rich, and extensive experience having created three educational enterprises that scaled successfully and led them as well as an additional fourth organization. From this experience, spanning decades and reflecting work with hundreds of people in the teams he built to run four large education enterprises serving thousands of children and youth, Earl distills key lessons that walk the reader through the process of creating an education organization. In clear and direct prose, each chapter conveys the essential elements of the seven building blocks which form the narrative arc of the book. The general principles are illustrated with examples drawn from Earl's extensive experience as an education entrepreneur. Each chapter concludes with key takeaways, providing a summary of the actionable steps covered.

In the course on educational innovation and social entrepreneurship I have taught at the Harvard Graduate School of Education for almost two decades, I have used a range of books and articles to cover the key concepts and tools students need to develop a business plan to sustain an education organization that will advance a particular education purpose. The book Earl Phalen has written stands in a class of its own for its direct and clear treatment of the subject, completeness in covering the key themes, and for the engaging and lively prose.

Every aspiring education entrepreneur, as well as those currently leading education entrepreneurial ventures, would benefit from reading this book. First to be reminded of what the essential building blocks are in creating and running a successful education enterprise, but just as important, to remember why creating and leading enterprises that truly advance educational opportunities for all is so necessary to sustain justice and democracy.

Fernando M. Reimers
Ford Foundation Professor of the Practice of International Education
Harvard Graduate School of Education

# Table of Contents

# Introduction

—▬—

Experience is the best teacher. There's nothing equal to the power of truly seeing, hearing, feeling, and living with something first-hand. But experience can only be gained in real time. And there are so many pressing issues and meaningful opportunities surrounding us today that your time is far too precious to squander.

I've written this book for aspiring and early stage entrepreneurs like you who have a vision for a better, more just society. After decades as a social impact leader with a solid track record of success, I'm sharing my experience in the hope of helping you avoid years of fruitless experimenting and misdirection. Or worse yet, falling short of your ambition and giving up on your dream because you've run out of time, money, or faith in yourself.

Throughout my life I have been nurtured, inspired, and supported by so many caring individuals---my family, our neighbors in my blue collar hometown, teachers, community activists, and leaders from many walks of life, each of whom helped me believe that big aspirations could be achieved (my personal evolution is explored in greater detail in my autobiography entitled "Giving My All").

In my professional life I have had the privilege of working with many gifted people who have pushed me to be and do more than I could ever have imagined or accomplished on my own. I'm humbled by what we have been able to achieve. I've been honored – as a result of being a part of great teams -- to receive numerous accolades including the President's Service Award from President Clinton, the BET National Hero Award, and the NCAA's Silver Anniversary Award. Yet there remains a great need for continued bold leadership in the social impact sector.

I have been extremely fortunate in the people who have shown up for me. But I have also found valuable guidance from my own personal research. As the only Black child adopted by the most loving Irish Catholic family, there were some parts of my history that I wasn't aware of until I got much older. In college, I came across a series called *Black Pioneers* – simple pamphlets offering brief biographies of Black thinkers, leaders, and scientists. This series introduced me to accomplished Black men such as Lewis Latimer, who helped create the lightbulb; Garrett Morgan, who invented the traffic light; and many others whose names have nearly been lost to history. I had the benefit of an excellent education, but I had no idea these Black heroes existed. I went on to read the speeches of the Civil Rights leaders, Martin Luther King Jr., Malcolm X, and their peers. What stood out so starkly was that each of these heroes worked against seemingly insurmountable odds in a society that largely chose to ignore, suppress, denigrate or even assassinate them.

Their examples gave me the inspiration to design my own vision for tackling an enduring injustice. I dreamed of creating a network of schools dedicated to serving Black and brown children in some of the poorest communities in America. Schools that would offer these unfairly undervalued children, my brothers and sisters, the education they deserved – an education that included instilling them with pride in their heritage and their humanity. This vision eventually formed the basis for my life's work.

In this book I offer readers the insights I didn't have when I chose the path to becoming a social entrepreneur and a leader in this space as a Black man. There are plenty of business books offering advice, but my story is meant for people who fall outside the traditional entrepreneurial investment circles, men and women of color, white women and low-income white men, especially those who wish to make a positive impact in underserved communities. Each chapter illustrates a major lesson I've learned about how to create and sustain an enterprise, complete with descriptions of my many setbacks and mistakes. My approach is not to give you a step-by-step plan but to propose seven guiding principles that I wish I had known earlier in my own journey.

My hope is that you can turn to these principles throughout your entrepreneurial career when you are at a roadblock, feeling confused, or full of doubt. Or maybe when you need reassurance that your challenges are not unique and that your setbacks can be significant opportunities for innovation.

Experience is a powerful teacher, but there's no reason for the next generation of social entrepreneurs to feel that they are solo pioneers with nothing to guide them. Just as I have benefitted from learning about the lives of those leaders who have gone before me, I hope you will take encouragement and practical advice from my story so that your path to meaningful achievement is both shorter and smoother.

# Chapter 1
# Commit to Your "Why"

———————

*"Find your why and you'll find your way." -John C. Maxwell*

We are all attracted by certainties. Questions make us uncomfortable. But making the effort to answer hard questions is where we find real meaning.

I began searching for my "why" when my college girlfriend asked a question that stumped me. At the time I was enjoying life as a Yale undergraduate. I had plenty of opinions and the youthful confidence that I already knew lots of answers. So, when she asked, "what is your purpose in life?" I wanted to shoot back a cool reply. Instead, all I could do was blink and think, stalling for time. I guess I managed to say something but it sure wasn't memorable or true. It got me asking myself the tough questions I hope anyone reading this book is asking. Why am I on this earth? What are the talents that are uniquely strong in me? What areas for growth are uniquely mine? How do I build a meaningful life from my answers?"

If you are looking for your "why", reflection and honest introspection is where to begin. Your "why" needs to bring out strong emotions in you. It might be anger or joy or a hope that your life can make a difference. Your "why" should make you feel whole because it expresses everything that you contain—your intellect, your heart, your creativity, your beliefs. Your "why" should create what Napoleon Hill refers to as a *burning desire*[1] inside of you.

It's no accident that every child's favorite word—after "no", of course—is "why". We become thinking human beings by trying to make

---

[1] https://www.goodreads.com/book/show/30186948-think-and-grow-rich

sense of the world. In fact, to a large extent we are all the result of other people's "whys."

I'd like to use my personal and professional story as an example of how I came to realize and be directed by my "why". I hope that my experiences can help you find, act on, and stay true to your own unique and precious "why".

## OPW- other people's "why"

In 1967 I was born to an eighteen year old woman who had the courage to admit she was unprepared to care for me. Her "why" probably was wanting a better life for her son than she could provide. I was placed into foster care and spent my first two years moving from one foster home to another.

I remember when my social worker, Fran, took me out for my favorite treat, strawberry ice cream, and introduced me to a man and woman who played with me in a nearby park. We tossed a ball around for a while before they bought me another favorite food, a hot dog. It was a fun afternoon, and it was easy for me to say yes when Fran asked if I'd like to see that man and woman again.

That man and woman, George and Veronica Phalen, soon became my adoptive parents. They welcomed me into their warm, loving household, which was already lively with seven of their biological children. Their "why" is simple and yet deep. Both of my parents were raised during the Great Depression, a time that helped shape their values of integrity, thrift, and a sense of responsibility for their neighbors. They were actively religious people who lived their lives according to the principles of the Catholic Church. They were also acutely aware of the struggle for civil rights led by Dr. Martin Luther King, Jr. in the 1960s. My mom in particular felt motivated to support equal justice for all Black Americans. With seven children at home, she couldn't go off to join the Freedom Riders in Alabama, but when she read a newspaper article stating that 70% of Black boys in the Massachusetts foster care system would end up in prison by age 21, she had an idea. The Phalens could adopt a Black boy. My dad agreed. They named me Earl Martin Phalen to honor Dr. Martin Luther King. Their "why"? All God's children deserve love, and if they could provide this love to another child they would do that.

There is no telling how my life would have gone differently if George and Veronica Phalen hadn't followed their "why".

Over the early years of my life and education, I encountered many other wonderful people acting on their "why". But the "why" that put me on my career and life journey was the question that came from a little girl living in an orphanage in Jamaica.

By this time, I had completed my first year at Harvard Law School and I was struggling with decisions about what career direction to take in life. Some sort of public service appealed to me, so I signed up for a summer internship with an international social justice organization in Jamaica. The work was powerful, but I wanted the chance to work with children, so I found a volunteer opportunity at a local orphanage. My first day there, I showed up expecting to help out one of the teachers, only to be told the teacher had just quit. I had to lead the class of 21 children myself. No plan, no preparation. Just me and 42 young eyes staring at me expectantly as I walked to the front of the classroom.

The kids helped me out by telling me what their routine usually was. It started with a math session.

OK, I can do this, I thought. Then one of the littlest kids, a girl with a loose tooth and shiny braids, called me over to her workbook. "Mr. Earl," she asked, "what's one plus one?" "Well," I said, "one plus one is two. Why?" the wide-eyed girl asked.

While I tried to figure out what to say, an older girl walked over with a handful of crayons. She put one on the table and asked how many crayons were there. "One," the little girl said. The teen placed another crayon next to it. "Now how many?"

"Two?" the girl replied uncertainly.

"That's right" the teen assured her. The little girl broke into a wide grin, then looked at me and asked, "Give me another problem."

"Okay, what is 2 + 1?" I said.

"You take 2 crayons," she explained, "and add them to one crayon, and then count them all. One, two, three. *Three*!" she announced, this time with real confidence.

"I am smart!" she said beaming.

"That's correct" I replied, "you are so smart."

She was smart. I knew it and now she knew it. This was it. I had just seen someone demonstrate the tremendous impact of learning. This young scholar wasn't just imitating someone else– she understood the process and experienced the rush of joy and empowerment it brought her. I knew then that I wanted every child to have this transformative moment. I knew it would be my "why" ---- helping children find their power through education.

## Going where your "why" takes you

I wish I could say that once I found my "why", or it found me, I stepped onto a straight path leading directly to success. Not so. For starters my parents were understandably concerned, maybe even alarmed when I called them collect from Jamaica and announced, "I'm dropping out of law school to become a teacher. I need to stop wasting time and teaching is what I believe I am called to do." Their silence was my first hurdle. A bit of backstory will help explain the moment.

When I was in the 3$^{rd}$ grade I started to take an interest in social justice. As only a somewhat precocious third grader can reason, I settled on a goal to become the mayor of a city as the best way to make the world a better place. For many years afterwards whenever any adult asked what I wanted to be when I grew up my answer came without hesitation. "I'm going to be a mayor."

People came to refer to me as "the kid who plans to run for mayor."

Partly with this aspiration in mind and largely because I followed in my brother David's footsteps, I studied political science in college and then expected to get a law degree as preparation for a career in public office. My parents never expressed a specific opinion about my ambitions. They made it clear they mostly wanted me to be happy, and like most parents they hoped I would achieve my full potential.

Naturally, then, when I decided to defer going to Harvard Law School for a year so that I could join the Lutheran Volunteer Corps they questioned my choice but supported me. I moved to Washington, DC where I assumed responsibility as the Assistant Coordinator at Luther Place Shelter, an organization which provided a safe living space for homeless women hoping to transition to full-time housing. My salary was $85 a month. Working at the shelter was one of the best years of my life. That may be hard to believe when the job consisted of working 100 hours a week in a world of drug addiction, prostitution, mental illness and broken families. Still, it was a beautiful community where my Birkenstock wearing, vegetarian co-workers wanted everything we consumed-- food, TV, music, media—to be healthy for mind, body and spirit. What I gained in being part of this beautiful community and learning more about myself made up for the low wages. Living in a genuine community with my colleagues and the women at the shelter proved to me that I love working directly with those I am here to serve.

After that year in DC, I took my place at Harvard Law and got through an exhausting first year. Then came my time in Jamaica and my conviction that pursuing a career as a lawyer was not for me. But stepping off the lawyer's career path by dropping out of Harvard did not strike my parents as a smart move. They wanted me to complete my degree. Their advice was reasoned, calm, and loving. A degree from Harvard Law would open doors for me for the rest of my life. I couldn't know what I might want to do in the future – why not keep all my options open? And they were right. I returned to law school for my second year but this time it was with a mission in mind. I knew I would build a career not just in some form of direct service but specifically in education. Staying in law school didn't derail my "why". It helped me figure out my next steps.

After returning from Jamaica, I looked for a way to continue teaching. With a group of like-minded classmates, I signed up for an after school mentoring program through the Boys and Girls Club in Roxbury, Massachusetts. Mentors spent one day a week helping middle-schoolers with homework and projects. A second day was meant as a hangout time, sharing pizza and games with the kids. It only took one day of tutoring for us to discover how terribly behind these kids were in basic reading, writing, and math skills. We knew pizzas and homework help wasn't going to give these youngsters the boost they needed to get a decent education. Fueled with equal parts enthusiasm and naivete, my friends and I formed my first non-profit, BELL. BELL, which stood for Building Educated Leaders for Life, was named in honor of the incredible Professor Derrick Bell.[2] Through the process of establishing and then leading BELL, I realized my "why" was changing. While I loved teaching, I began to see how much greater an impact I could have through entrepreneurship---by building an organization to reach many more children.

Instead of holding on to my original vision of becoming a teacher, I saw an opportunity to better leverage my strengths to have a powerful impact. And I went for it with BELL.

I soon discovered my new "why" meant acquiring many entrepreneurial skills. Taking full advantage of my years in law school, I learned how to fundraise, the crucial importance of cultivating and maintaining relationships, and what it means to squarely face what you don't know and humbly learn by trial and error.

Over the long course of my career, I have faced these moments of opportunity and choice many, many times. What has proven most useful to my decision making has been coming back to my "why" and asking if it would be better served by taking a different route than I had originally planned. Part of your responsibility as an entrepreneur is to see opportunity, perhaps where no one else sees it yet. If it aligns with your "why", even when it is not what others think you should do, your job is to go down the new road your "why" points you to.

---

[2] Derrick Bell, legal scholar and teacher, was the first Black law professor at Harvard Law School to achieve tenure and one of the first African American deans in a non-historically Black law school. Bell was also a founder of an academic model called critical race theory. More on Dr. Bell

# Staying true to your "why"

Trusting your "why" is easier said than done. Yes, I believe listening to your intuition, trusting your "gut" is good advice. But putting yourself in situations that test your intuition and give you real experience matter even more.

If I had not done that volunteer year at the shelter, I would have been less prepared for taking the bigger step to my summer internship in Jamaica. My law school friends were doing internships in law firms, making good money and forming connections that might well lead to great jobs after graduation. My Jamaica experience started out in legal services but my desire to be of service led me to commit my time to an orphanage. My gut may have told me to make the change but my joy in the work was what confirmed for me that I was finding my "why".

Of course, it's one thing to choose service over salary while you are still a student. But soon I had to face a bigger decision: committing to a viable career. During my third year at Harvard Law, I received an offer from a San Francisco law firm to join them as an associate. They offered me a salary of $125,000 to start, quite a hefty sum in 1993. All I had to do was say yes.

Meanwhile I had this dream of what I wanted to do with BELL. It's not hard to imagine how this conversation went with my parents. I reminded my parents that they raised us all with the belief that "tomorrow is not promised." Passionately I tried to convince my parents of the urgency I felt. "I have to pursue my calling today...not tomorrow, today." My mom's practical side had to ask, "how are you going to live? Why not consider taking the law job, making good money for many years, and then doing some social good?" It's a persuasive argument, especially for people of color and those fortunate enough to be the first generation to earn a college degree. If you're the first, there's tremendous pressure to take the traditional route to wealth through a prestigious career. Earn first, then give back.

My parents lovingly told me why turning down the associate's position was a really bad idea. I had $125,000 in one hand, and in the other a $12,500 grant I'd won from the Echoing Green foundation to further develop BELL.

If I chose BELL, after paying another staff member and program costs, my salary for the first year would be $5,000. With the law job, eventually I'd make it to partner, earn $750,000 a year, and change my future family's life for generations to come.

The number of zeroes represented a "fork in the road" decision—just one example of the type of choices you will have to make during your career. That meager $12,500 grant was a punch in the jaw that woke me up to a hard reality. If I picked the BELL option I would be committing to running a nonprofit business without knowing anything about finance, strategy, recruitment, management---basically anything that qualified me for a leadership role. Because I grew up comfortably, I was blessed with a mindset that enabled me not to worry about having money and things. My spirituality and my passion for justice also helped me believe that if I do the right thing, if the work I choose makes the world a better place, then God would protect me. But He's not going to do the work for me.

## Why even have a "why"?

The life of an entrepreneur is difficult, and especially hard for people who fall outside the traditional idea of an entrepreneur - people of color, women, and people from underserved communities. You will confront discrimination, institutional barriers, and a conventional business infrastructure that seems unwilling to take you seriously or invest money in your ideas. There will be setbacks, catastrophes, plenty of mistakes, and most definitely outright failures.

I can't know what your "why" is, but I know that especially for many entrepreneurs who are people of color, women, or from underserved communities, the depths of pain you see in the world matters. Every person in this world has experienced pain. Everywhere you look there are reminders that we had better give our best because otherwise the suffering remains pervasive and intractable. Even today it's impossible to ignore racial hatred so in your face that it snaps you back to reality. I was watching *Till* (the film portraying Emmitt Till's tragic story) the other day, and I felt an overwhelming need to apologize that I haven't done more to address blatant racism – and done it faster and better. As a social entrepreneur there are a lot of reminders that the fight you wage had better be fierce.

You will face challenges today even more daunting than what I had to overcome decades ago.

Without a "why" it is unthinkable, even impossible to keep going. As it did for me, your "why" might evolve and take different shapes. Those you rely on during your journey may also evolve, the folks you need to help you problem solve. I can never express enough gratitude to the advisors and mentors who taught me how to do so much and who helped me survive the emotional challenges you go through as a leader. These people understood my "why", helped me stay grounded, and accelerated my growth with their support. Without these mentors and advisors, the constant barrage of problems we all have to face as entrepreneurs could have extinguished that fire that was my "burning desire."

## You are worthy

Too often I hear early stage entrepreneurs say about their enterprise "it's so hard to have one school. I just *hope* I can get to two." Depending on hope and setting your sights too low can seriously limit your ability to be successful. It reminds me of my first year of law school when I overheard two students talking about getting A's when I and some of my peers were saying we hoped we would just make it through the year. Beliefs do matter. We must search out role models from *all* backgrounds who are doing work we admire. Look at what they have been able to do. Ask yourself "what would it take for me to do that, too?" You've got to be around the people who are aiming for A's – or honest enough to express it.

If as entrepreneurs we do not set our thermostat high for what's possible and do that by looking at the best, the biggest, the most successful, we will never do more than get through the year. Set your imagination free. Part of what I want to encourage you to do is to keep imagining bigger—ask yourself, "what would I need to grow--- advisors, capital, access?" Study the behaviors and key performance metrics and achievements of the most successful organizations, both inside and outside of your sector. It's no secret there is systematic racism in capital access—who gets money and who doesn't. And sometimes a small part of the problem is our sense that we are not worthy to ask. When I became the CEO of KC Scholars we approached the Ewing Marion Kaufmann Foundation and asked for a quarter of a billion dollars -- $250M– in funding. Based on feedback, we later lowered our ask to up to $187M in three performance-based installments. And we got it. But we wouldn't have if we hadn't been bold enough and confident enough and felt we were deserving enough to ask. Imagination and belief in your "why" are critical parts of success.

*Finding your "why"* starts by asking yourself, "If I had no fear, what would I do? Quit my job and launch my dream venture, write a book, travel the world?" It's essential to take time to reflect and honestly answer these types of questions. As Simon Sinek shows in his Golden Circle illustration[3], your "why" gets built from the inside out. The outer ring is WHAT you plan to do, the middle ring is HOW you plan to do it, but the core, at the very heart of every endeavor is the most potent motivator, the WHY.

*Following your "why"* involves the rocking chair test. If you live to be 80 or 100 and your great grandkids ask you "what did you do that you're most proud of?" what will you say? At the end of your days don't be stumped by that question that set me on my quest so long ago. You want to be able to assure those young souls, "I know why I was put on this earth."

---

[3] https://simonsinek.com/golden-circle/

**Key Takeaways**

1.  Only you can define your why and when you do, it should create a 'burning desire' inside of you.

2.  As you face tough decisions, staying true to your "why" will guide you.

3.  When you set your sights on accomplishment, don't settle for getting by. Always aim high.

# Chapter 2
# Find Your People

—▬—

*"None of us, acting alone, can achieve success." - Nelson Mandela*

## The Myth of Bootstrapping

I am proud to be a leader, but I am not a self-made man. Anyone who claims they "made it on their own" through hard work and exceptional skill may be kidding themselves, but I'm not fooled, and you shouldn't be either. Just as I can point to all the Other People's Whys that helped shape me as a person, I can readily name a long list of people who at various critical times in my life and career gave me just what I needed to succeed. Luck plays a part in every business venture, but don't count on being lucky. Count on people.

My work and life experiences have shown me that there are three essential elements behind every truly successful venture:

1.  A good idea (notice I say "good." Great is better, but often "good" is enough.)

2.  A business model with a financial engine that enables growth/scale

3.  The right people in the right roles

Later in this book I'll share what I've learned about the importance of good ideas and business models, but this chapter is all about what I wholly believe is *the greatest determinant of your success---your people.* It might surprise you to know that people help you in many ways, even sometimes by challenging your ideas or saying "no" when you want to hear "yes." Included in my list of most influential people are those who supported me, advised me, and encouraged me, but also those who at key moments confronted me with hard truths. These include my parents, siblings and closest friends; educators and community leaders such as my English teacher at Norwood High School, Dave Powell; long time civil rights activist, Ruth Batson who I had the honor to know; the Jesse Climenko Professor at Harvard Law School, Charles Ogletree, Jr.; Harvard University chief development officer, Bayley Mason; Harvard School of Education professor, Dr. Robert Peterkin, and so many more. Some of these names will appear later in this account but all of them have been powerfully influential in my life. Before I offer proof of how key individuals have made my success possible, let's explore the why and how for the foundation of your efforts to find your people.

## Why Not Go It Alone?

Even the most talented among us can't excel at everything. Remember Michael Jordan's early NBA Championship ambitions? We all need other people (Scottie Pippen, Phil Jackson, Dennis Rodman), because each of us has certain skills and strengths but a healthy, thriving, superior organization needs a broader and a deeper skill set than any one individual can provide.

There's a saying making the rounds that captures this truth and I'm paraphrasing it here-- "You'll go faster alone, but you'll go farther with others." Every entrepreneur has a limited supply of resources, beginning with time, skills, and money. If you're not moving fast enough, you're most likely going to run out of money. Seeking advice from people whose life experience and chosen practice is relevant to your business is like adding accelerant to your pace. The right advisors are going to give you guidance that is ten, twenty, or even fifty years ahead of what you're thinking. If you ask the right questions and listen humbly and carefully, you can leverage their infinite wisdom. Honestly, following that practice has saved me from wasting many years making needless missteps. (And I have made more than enough missteps, but they helped me avoid making so many more.) Especially when you're starting out, but at every critical juncture in your business, making mistakes that could have been avoided can cause you to run out of time and money.

Asking for help from Bayley Mason offers one example of how

someone's deep knowledge and generosity propelled me forward. My young colleagues and I were still in law school, looking to launch BELL. We needed money and we had quickly exhausted the tactics we were familiar with for raising capital, like having fundraising parties. It became clear that, while successful, the events we were able to hold weren't going to bring in the capital we needed. Bayley Mason was leading the development efforts for Harvard University and had a tremendous track record for attracting billions in donations. I figured "why not ask someone who is amazingly successful and see what they can tell me?" Bayley kindly granted me a short interview and handed me a copy of *How to Fundraise*. "Read this," he said, "and come back later to discuss it."

I studied that book like it was a law text and came back to him with highlighted sections, notes, and lots of questions. He seemed surprised to see me but my willingness to do the preliminary work made him willing to coach me. Over a number of sessions and in fact for years afterwards, Bayley gave me the wisdom he had learned through decades of fundraising---a cram course in effective strategy, tactics, and procedures. His advice became my playbook for raising money. Maybe, years later, I would have eventually figured it out on my own, but I have no doubt Bayley prepared me to enter the field ready to play. And his coaching paid off immediately by improving my success rate with potential donors.

It might seem daunting to wonder who you can find to help you along. But wherever you are starting from -- no matter your age, your background, or your neighborhood -- I believe the right people exist who will want to help and will give you the advice or assistance you need to achieve your goals. Start where you are. Look around you—you may be closer than you think to a possible mentor for the skills and advice you need the most.

## Who Should I Ask for Help?

Before you start asking for help, be clear about what it is you need. Two activities will help you decide: honest reflection and informed feedback. Most of us know what we're good at. We've seen the results of our efforts and others have recognized our ability. Then there are the things we're able to do, but not well and not with much enthusiasm.

Tasks that you do because they have to be done and there's no one else to do them generally offer an indication of where you need help. It might be building a budget, making a pitch deck, or developing marketing materials for prospective customers. Start looking for people who have the skills you lack.

Sometimes we may enjoy doing something and even think we're pretty good at it, until someone sets us straight with some blunt feedback. My friend Terra Smith did that for me. As a leader at Summer Advantage, I knew that I was not good at hiring, yet as my organization was growing quickly I needed to keep adding talent. Without knowing it, historically, I had made important hiring decisions more because I liked the person and thought they'd be good to work with than because I had a clear notion of how their specific skills fit our business needs. Meanwhile my close friend Terra was doing hiring in a very different way. She was working as an attorney for a Wall Street law firm that recognized it needed to do more to improve the diversity of its talent pool. As a Black woman, Terra believed she could devise and implement a plan enabling her firm to attract top talent from HBCUs (Historically Black Colleges and Universities) and other sources. Terra did the job so expertly that other businesses started asking her to recruit for them. She left the law firm and launched a very successful consultancy around recruiting the best of the best for Wall Street companies that had ambitions to improve their position on DEI (Diversity Equity, Inclusion). So, when Terra looked at my hiring practices, she saw the weakness. I was hiring more on personality. Terra had honed her ability to hire based on matching a candidate's demonstrated performance with the skills a given position required. Using my less discerning approach, I was only scoring 50% in terms of identifying strongly impactful talent and retaining high performers. Pretty dismal and a big waste of time, money, and emotional capital.

"Earl," she began, "you're good at a whole lot of things, but hiring talent is definitely not one of them. Let me take it over." At first it stings a bit to be told you're failing, but the facts are the facts. Later on, I learned about Henry Ford's hiring and retention criteria, what he referred to as Q.Q.S. Every new hire at *any* level in the organization needs to hit the mark for **Quality** of work, **Quantity** of work, and **Spirit** of work. You can be a prolific producer, churning out high quality work, but grumbling and grousing the whole time. No good. Or you're a warm, friendly person who everyone likes to be around, but your work is subpar. Also, no good. I was hiring people while hoping for the best, instead of evaluating them based on clarity around what needed to be done, what it would take to accomplish it, what our culture looked for in personal style, and how we measured success for that position.

Being able to turn the hiring responsibilities over to someone I trusted, who aligned with the vision, values, and mission of my organization, was a relief and a blessing. Terra's ability to find the right person for the right position meant her new hires had an immediate (and lasting) positive impact on the organization. We grew stronger and faster because I got out of the way.

When you're building your enterprise, look for purposeful, impact-oriented people who also have a strong "why" and skills different from your own. If you turn the hiring decisions over to someone else, "delegate but don't abdicate." I learned to utilize the TopGrading[4] process of talent selection. Terra led and had all final decision-making power, while I also had a framework to make me a better partner in the process. Make sure the expectations and success metrics are firmly in place and are routinely being revisited.

## Where Do I Find Allies?

Sometimes if you are really lucky, the help you need comes from your inner circle, people like Terra who are already in your life. But most of the time you need to and should look beyond those you already know well. One thing to remember if you struggle to overcome your reluctance to approach strangers is that most successful people recognize the help they were given when they were coming up. They want to repay that kindness by lending a hand to the next generation.

If you are in a college or university setting, look across all of the resources within the school, not just people in your major or department.

---

[4] Hiring practice methodology

Harvard Development Director, Bayley Mason had no obligation to help a law student, but he went above and beyond because I asked and showed I was serious. I never took a class with the distinguished Harvard law professor Charles Ogletree, but because I sought out his advice, he did more for me than anyone except my family members had ever done.

Use the power of the internet and media to identify people whose work earns your respect and admiration. After I watched the documentary, "Eyes on the Prize" I was inspired by the dynamic civil rights activist, Ruth Batson. When I tried to find out more about her I was stunned to discover that she lived in the Boston area. I sent her a note (this was before email), and she agreed to meet me. It was the beginning of a rich, rewarding relationship with an elder I looked up to.

Don't be afraid to use respectful direct outreach. Are there people in your city, in your religious community, in similar organizations, or in your business community whose work you admire? Tell them "I'm so inspired by what you do. Can I meet with you to learn more about how you do what you do?" Go to relevant events, conferences, and professional gatherings with a plan in mind. It's not enough to just attend. Study the list of speakers, decide who you would like to meet, figure out what you want to say to them, and then make it happen. Especially in the early days I would routinely set myself goals for attending such sessions---how many contacts did I want to make, who were the people I wanted to meet, what could I do to make the event worthwhile? I would envision the results that defined success before attending meetings and events.

The internet and social media make finding inspiration easier than ever: TED talks, videos, blogs, podcasts. These can be sources for "virtual" advisors, learning from people who you may never meet but whose message speaks to you and offers useful insights.

No matter how you manage to connect with people whose help you seek, the most critical piece is *following through*. Don't just file that person's card in a drawer. Email, text, or call them with an invitation for coffee or lunch or dinner. If I hadn't come back to Bayley Mason's office after reading the book he gave me, I would never have received the valuable education he offered. Had I not sent a hand written thank you note within 24 hours of meeting him, he might not have accepted my next request to meet.

Showing that the person genuinely matters to you is the way to begin to build a relationship. Be honest about what you need, do your homework in advance, know what to ask for, and always remember to say thank you.

## What If People Tell Me Something I Don't Want to Hear

Earlier I mentioned that it takes all sorts of people to help you succeed. We often think "help" only takes the form of being consistently positive and supportive of everything we do. But for you to mature as a leader and for your organization to outperform the competition you also have to hold space for people who aren't afraid to challenge you--- the knowledgeable people who will engage in rigorous debate around critical decisions and force you to think about what might happen in the future.

One memorable conversation with George Overholser brought this home to me.

After a promising start, the organization that I had founded and was leading, BELL, was struggling to pay its bills. The No Child Left Behind (NCLB) federal legislation had been approved, earmarking millions for tutoring programs for children living in low-income communities. We wanted to qualify for this funding because we knew it could support future growth and success for BELL.

But we faced a huge problem. Our business model deviated significantly from NCLB's operating specifications. BELL took pride in our extremely low 1 to 3 tutor to student ratio. Our tutors were undergraduate and graduate students with a passion for youth education. The program ran for 36 weeks, from 3-6pm each weekday, delivering not just critical learning skills but providing mentoring and much needed full after school daycare to families. Everyone on staff at BELL led with empathy and lived by the motto that "*Kids don't care how much you know until they know how much you care.*"

NCLB only funded programs staffed by certified teachers at a 1 to 8 ratio, running for only 28 weeks, and offering a short day of 2.5 hours of instruction. Pivoting to conform to this model meant hiring and training an entirely new set of tutors – namely certified teachers -- upping the compensation, altering the student/tutor ratio, changing the curriculum to fit the shorter day, and seriously reducing the long childcare hours families had come to rely on. In short it was like destroying our proven program model and designing a new one nearly from scratch. The proverbial "building the plane while flying it" scenario. Still, I had to face the reality that as much as we considered our current model a success, it wasn't financially sustainable.

My process was to discuss our options with everyone. It was like a mental ping-pong game of back and forth, pros and cons. I wasn't getting anywhere, and it felt like the decision was never going to make itself.

After weeks of wavering, I was sitting at the donated mahogany desk in my small office on the 2$^{nd}$ floor of the BELL offices going over a PowerPoint presentation that laid out the options and possible consequences. In walked George Overholser, a consultant for one of our donor institutions, New Profit Inc., and an advisor I had come to rely on for his calm, cerebral coaching style. I walked George through the presentation and my narration kept coming back to the same place. I just kept saying "I think we should do what it takes to go for the NCLB funding, but I'm worried. If we lose the college kids' passion, renege on the daycare hours for parents, increase our student headcount, we'll lose our identity." I kept restating the problem. It was clear to George I was stuck.

Normally a soft-spoken man, George suddenly snapped forward in his desk chair. "Earl, you have got to make a decision," he fired at me. "Decision making requires a mental muscle. Yours seems to have gotten weak and you don't want to exercise it." His strong words woke me up.

He told me that "all leaders face decisions with uncertain outcomes and incomplete information. Naturally you're going to worry about the consequences. But stop worrying and start planning. How can you mitigate the risks for the best of two challenging options?"

It was embarrassing to be caught waffling for so long. But as soon as I made the decision I felt a fundamental change in my leadership skills.

Deciding to rework our entire business model meant figuring out how to build a new model that preserved what we cherished about our original approach. If we're worried about leading with emotion and empathy, how do we build it into the new teacher job description? If we're concerned the larger student/tutor ratio won't be as effective, how will we ensure it will be? We looked at every aspect of our program and organization, and revised or amended it to make sure we would still be able to reach our goals using the NCLB specifications. To the parents who were losing some daycare hours, we explained the reason behind our decision. They realized that the greatest value our program delivered wasn't daycare. It was developing their children's writing and reading skills and their confidence that they were scholars.

George's firm directive pushed me to a new level of leadership and that big, hard decision plus lots of creative reimagining by my team made all the difference for BELL. We secured No Child Left Behind funding, then quickly grew from a $2M organization to $4M, then $9M, and on to $27M. Most importantly, our program outcomes soared. And we could measure our growth not only by additional revenue but by the vastly increased number of children and families we were able to serve. Our success using our re-designed business model became the basis for additional legislation, the STEP UP Act, authorized by then Senator Barack Obama. George was so right. Leaders have to make hard decisions first, then get to work making sure the things they fear might go wrong, don't.

An important practice Professor Ogletree and my brothers Jimmy and David taught me is how to "disagree without being disagreeable." I used to think I had to convince naysayers that I was right. I've learned instead to listen. People who shoot holes in my plans are giving me a gift. They are raising objections I need to know how to answer. Instead of shutting them down I've learned to ask them to tell me everything that is possibly flawed with my approach. After thanking them, I'll go away and get with my team to come up with a counterstrategy for each weak point. There's no need to change the naysayer's mind, even loving naysayers. Change your plan to bulletproof it instead.

There will come a time when you receive lots of conflicting or contradictory advice from the many sources in your network. Being confronted by an overwhelming difference of opinions can push you into "paralysis by analysis." You find yourself simply unable to choose. So many of my family members and mentors showed me that staying true to my core values and vision provides the necessary guidance for sound decision making.

Most of the time you will be asked to decide between two "best" choices, neither of which is optimum. List the pros and cons, socialize your thoughts with informed, trusted people, then stop waffling. Choose your course of action. Start designing how you will reduce each risk. What key performance indicators (KPIs), quarterly goals, or other benchmarks can you put in place to help you stay on track? Each time you put yourself through the tough process of decision-making you are exercising that leadership muscle. And as with any regular exercise, it will make you and your organization stronger.

## What Can I Offer Those Who Help?

You can't put a price on wisdom. When I reflect on the precious gifts of insight, knowledge and advice so many have freely given me I am humbled and forever grateful. By helping me, many of my mentors and benefactors have felt the satisfaction of repaying a debt they may feel they owed to their own mentors. In truth, most human beings feel better giving help when and where we can, paying it forward to see the next generation succeed.

When you are the recipient of such generosity, be sure to thank the person in meaningful ways. The rule of thumb I practice is *3 for 1*---for every kindness I receive, I try to express my gratitude in 3 different, equally sincere ways. For example, when someone gives me something I have asked them for, whether it's a donation, information, or a "warm" referral, I want them to know what that has meant for me and the organization. I don't just say "thank you." In an email or note I may share what happened as a result---we were able to fund 10 more scholarships, we secured the contract you advised us on, we partnered with the business you connected us with to sponsor a big new community event. After the email I'll follow up again several weeks or months later with another update and progress report. I make a point to keep the dialogue alive, acknowledging the continued success they have helped bring about. It is true. It is authentic. Without advocates, the work of my organizations would not be possible. Pure gratitude coupled with hard data carries far more worth than mere money.

Cherish these relationships and nurture them with meaningful contact. A coffee date, lunch, or dinner on you provides a chance to report on new developments but also to continue to get to know each other better. Your supporters want to see the effects they are having. The more you can share about their impact, the more you show how deeply you value them, the more likely they are to continue to happily help you in any way they can.

As you plan to launch your business or grow it to the next level, my experience showed me that the decisions you make around people--- your team, your advisors, your board, your community partners, are the most critical choices you'll make. Don't make the mistake of surrounding yourself with your "clones" or with those who will only support your recommendations. To build your enterprise with resilience and excellence, commit yourself to finding purposeful, impact-oriented people who have a strong "why" but skills that are both different from and complementary to yours– people who aren't afraid to "disagree without being disagreeable." People who will push you to confront critical decisions that help shape the future in positive ways.

**Key Takeaways**

1. Take an honest inventory of your strengths and surround yourself with talent that fills any skill or knowledge gap.

2. Your success depends in large part on your ability to identify, recruit, retain and surround yourself with great people.

3. Look for allies and advisors and prepare thoughtful and informed ways to engage them.

4. Decision making is a muscle. Rarely will there be perfect information that leads to a perfect decision. Regardless, learning to make hard decisions will help you grow as a leader.

5. Find multiple, meaningful ways to express gratitude to your team and everyone who supports you.

# Chapter 3
# MAKE A PLAN

———————

*"I don't think there's a shortage of remarkable ideas... what's missing isn't the ideas. It's the will to execute them." Seth Godin*

If thinking about something were enough to make it happen, we'd all be getting a whole lot more done. In reality the gap between an *idea* and an *accomplishment* is huge. To bridge this daunting gap, you've got to have a plan. And be prepared to revise it and rework it and rethink it, again and again.

While this may sound painful, the real pain is in procrastination, missteps, and underdeveloped approaches that abruptly end in failure. I learned this lesson in college when early on I struggled to write a term paper that would at least be judged adequate. It wasn't because I didn't have ideas. Those I had in good supply. But getting them down on paper, that was the problem. Like all practiced procrastinators, I'd found many things to distract me or enable me to postpone committing my ideas to the page. When I finally got a sentence or two down, or maybe a few paragraphs, I'd read it over, decide it was awful, and delete it. Hours of this "no plan" approach got me nowhere. Time was running out before my paper was due.

My college friend and suitemate Jen Brown was a term paper writing whiz. When I watched her method for working on a paper, it was an impressive sight. Jen used a stack of index cards, each showing a key thought, a supporting quote, or evidence from our readings or the lectures. She spread them out on the dorm floor, arranging and rearranging them until she had the structure of her paper laid out in a way that explained and proved her argument. Then she started writing. The ideas and words seemed to flow effortlessly. One look at her process and I knew it wasn't going to work for me. It just wasn't my style. But I asked Jen for advice anyway.

"Earl, you have got to stop procrastinating," she insisted. "You need to just start writing and stop editing yourself after every line. Don't aim for perfection. Get everything you're thinking on paper without second guessing. Write the first version knowing that you're going to redo it 20 times."

It took a minute for that to sink in, but Jen wasn't done yet. "You're a terrific speaker and you've got a great ear for language. Once you've gotten that first draft on paper, read it out loud. You're going to hear what doesn't sound right. Fix it. After you've done that a bunch of times, you're going to have a paper that makes sense, reads well, and lays out a convincing argument." Now that sounded like something I could do.

Jen's advice helped me find *my* way to writing successful papers. But the larger lesson, about getting started with the understanding that *revising and rethinking* are where the real work takes place, that lesson informed the way I approach every new undertaking, beginning with the business planning process.

You will receive all sorts of conflicting advice about the importance of a business plan. After years of experimenting with a variety of approaches, I believe the discipline of writing a business plan creates value for the entrepreneur in many ways. First of all, it forces you to start building the bridge between your idea, your plan, and its execution. Without a detailed set of steps for executing on your vision, your chances of success are slim. Treat this plan like a rough draft. Keep reading, listening and rewriting. This process of iteration is a key way of testing your plan prior to implementation.

Next, your initial research, enhanced with feedback from other advisors and experts, will help you make a new version better than the first. To increase your chances of success, you want to keep iterating with input from others, making each version sharper, clearer and more attainable before you launch. If you skip or rush doing the hard work of accurately, effectively defining and describing your idea and its implementation plan, you won't have a way to interest investors, attract capital, and recruit the team you need to make the vision a reality.

The three key elements I look for in a polished, professional business plan are:

- A clear definition of the program, product, or service you plan to create along with an explanation of the "problem" or "pain point" it solves for your target audience.

- Professional profiles of the team who are going to make the vision happen, bios that emphasize what they have actually accomplished in the past and specific goals that they will individually and collectively achieve---not their past "activities" but the measurable results they achieved.

- A business model including financial forecasts that project how your organization will be sustained short term and fueled for long term growth.

Of course, there's more to it than that. Market/industry analysis and risk assessment need to be explored. A thoughtful SWOT (Strengths, Weaknesses, Opportunities, Threats) has to be folded in. The vision and mission statement for your organization should also be part of the building blocks for the enterprise. Solid business plans should indicate how you intend to measure performance, not just by bottom line results but more holistically as they reflect your mission and values. Two useful templates for building your internal business processes are the Balanced Scorecard[5] and the concept of SMART (Specific, Measurable, Achievable, Relevant, Time-based) goals. You can find tools to help at a variety of websites.[6]

Only through careful research will you be able to assemble this plan. And most importantly, though you need to work hard on this and make it the best you can, know you will need to revise it – in fact, be excited about how many times you will revise it -- as you learn more about the realities of your market and industry, and continue to solicit and

---

[5] https://www.investopedia.com/terms/b/balancedscorecard.asp

[6] https://www.indeed.com/career-advice/career-development/how-to-write-smart-goals

incorporate honest feedback from your advisors, experts and customers.

To help you get started I recommend Verne Harnish's short form business plan laid out in his excellent book, *Scaling Up.*

Sometimes this discipline of writing a business plan yields an unexpected upside. Although it was not projected in our business plan, PLA University is exceeding our expectations for growth and impact. The point is that business plans are not crystal balls. Even though they cannot reliably or infallibly predict the future, dedicating yourself to crafting the best version that you can while seeking out sound advice and incorporating it into a new iteration, these are the best practices that will give you the strongest foundation for launching any venture. As a wise non-profit entrepreneur who created a billion dollar enterprise once told me, "First comes vision, then comes provision."

## Refining the Plan "99 Times"

As a first time entrepreneur it's easy to fall into the trap of pursuing "uniqueness." Certainly, you will need to express specifically what it is about your business that sets you apart---your differentiation from the competition. But don't make the mistake of trying to be "unique" in every aspect. Lean fully into the fundamentals of the best businesses in your sector. You don't have to "invent" or "disrupt" how to do payroll or other standard operating procedures. Learn when the smart thing to do is copy others. Save the "innovations" for aspects of your business that will provide genuine strategic advantage. And always build on what you learn from watching and studying others. Ruki Neuhold-Ravikumar, CEO of the Kansas City Art Institute, once gave me this advice---that the best way to create something beautiful is to commit to "refining it 99 times."

When we launched the George and Veronica Phalen Leadership Academies (PLA) in 2013, we were able to take the many lessons we learned from studying other established charter school networks. We also had the benefit of insights gained over the 17 years of trial and error operating BELL. Between 2013 and 2021, PLA grew from 1 to 24 schools spanning Alabama, Indiana, Michigan, Ohio, Texas, and Washington, DC – and from impacting the lives of 124 scholars to 10,000 children. Our staff grew from 24 individuals to a team of over 1,200. The expertise I gained from BELL in programmatic and logistical leadership, fundraising and organizational development skills all contributed to a solid base. My team was strong. But even with the BELL experience, there was still much to learn for PLA.

In 6 months, a fast ideation process for a complex enterprise, we had a program plan for PLA schools. When we rolled it out, it wasn't at all like the general ideas we started with or anything else we had done before. For starters there were layers of rules and regulations we hadn't had to comply with in our earlier ventures. We spent six months really researching the programmatic elements of the best charter schools in the country. And we expanded our inquiry to look at other types of high performing schools across the nation. Our team worked to uncover the consistent obstacles to success other enterprises faced and how they overcame them or lessons we could glean from their failures. We analyzed all the practices we looked into, going really deep to discover what resources, approaches and processes were most likely to help us succeed. Even with all this information guiding us, we knew we were going to make mistakes.

What our experience showed us is that if you commit yourself to 99 times of revising and improving upon what you believe you want to build, you start to let your ideas and sense of possibilities flow freely. We remembered the lessons from when we launched and were attempting to scale BELL. Instead of settling on a standard operating approach, we played with the business model in a long series of iterations. We asked, "What would the BELL program look like if we operate it 1 day a week, what if we add another day, or 4 days a week, or even go to 5?" We played with every scenario. Should we have no set curriculum and instead focus on homework completion to build grade level skills? Or should remedial tutoring take precedence over homework since most of our scholars were performing 2-3 years below their grade level? Should we only use college students as tutors and mentors, or should we recruit experienced teachers? And what is the "right" tutor-to-mentor ratio? We got feedback from parents, teachers, and students on all the ideas we had. Their input plus allowing ourselves time to reflect regularly on our progress toward our goals allowed us to continuously improve our tutoring and mentoring program.

We used a similar but even more intense process with our schools, PLA. Methodical research into 57 schools and careful business modelling informed each iteration—and there were many of those.

PLA's systemized business planning gave us far deeper industry knowledge than we had ever compiled in our previous ventures. We felt armed with an understanding of what works and what doesn't in schools and education. Devoting time and resources to this research was a distinct departure from our earlier efforts, where often we were building things long after we should have had them in place. In our previous venture, BELL, we emphasized organizational learning while doing. With PLA we sought to learn as much as we could *before* the doing started.

Still, even with this extensively researched business plan, there was much more to learn. The insights we gained through structured reflection gave us an advantage when we planned our next initiative, PLA University, a tuition-free workforce development program for adults launched in 2020.

When we investigated other educational models for PLA schools, we asked all kinds of questions. My leadership team – Terra Smith, Johnny Jin and Eva Spilker – worked virtually and lived in different parts of the country. We used our geographic separation to our advantage, visiting and learning from the best schools in our region, for a total of 57 exceptional and varied schools. We organized our notes and shared them across the team, enabling us to identify common themes not only from charter schools but from the best schools of any kind in the country serving populations similar to and different from ours. The weakness in our method was that, while we identified the resources necessary for school success—for example, each high performing school had a great school leader—we didn't ask the more nuanced questions. We did not iterate 99 times. We didn't question if the DNA of a public school principal is different than that of a charter school principal, for instance. We didn't build detailed compensation, incentive, and retention plans that would best align with our impact plan. We didn't explore how we would onboard and train our leaders. It took us 7 years to recognize the necessary solution and decide to build our Principal Residency Program.

The same lack of deep understanding applies to creating an accurate profile for our ideal teachers. We didn't pull back and ask "what is the philosophical piece or motivation that prompts a teacher to want to go into a turnaround school in the toughest neighborhood in our cities? How is that different from a teacher who opts for the exclusive preparatory school offering average salary but above average amenities and bragging rights?" Only in retrospect did I realize we hadn't gone deep enough to understand how our generalities about the critical people and processes that contribute to successful educational enterprises needed to be refined in order to match our specific situation, needs, and ambitions.

In 2020, in the wake of George Floyd's murder, we launched PLA University, a short term training program available to anyone 17 years or older who is currently earning less than $45,000 a year. PLA U offers tuition-free professional skills workshops and credential programs that lead to securing jobs that pay on average between $45,000-$85,000 per year plus benefits. By the time we started planning PLA U we had come to understand from our experience at PLA schools that we needed to go deeper in our analysis of what factors contributed to success. For example, in the case of PLA schools, being a public school principal vs. a charter school principal is like the difference between being a franchise owner and operating a standalone company. Franchisees buy into a playbook with lots of established processes, support and infrastructure. The standalone operator is figuring it out and putting it together largely on their own. Typically, these two operators, even within the same industry, are going to have very different personality profiles. We missed that nuance in our PLA planning. For our next enterprise we knew we had to have a fuller understanding of the key success factors.

Had we made that breakthrough discovery while we were designing and iterating our operating model for PLA schools, our business plan would have veered in a different direction. We would have started off not by building the first school but by building a program to provide our critical, highly specific human resources. We would have launched a Principal Residency Program to train the leaders essential to a successful school. If we had put 2-3 people per one school leadership opportunity through a residency program preparing them for the things they would need to do in a PLA school, discussing and debriefing with them along the way, PLA would have had a significantly stronger start, and it would be double the size it is today.

At the industry level, even with our best efforts at understanding successful schools, we missed the whole notion of the science of student enrollment. The first year of our flagship PLA school, George and Veronica Leadership Academy, we had 541 applications. Hooray! We knew there'd be some drop off and we were prepared to lose a few of those scholars, maybe 10%. But on opening day when only 124 students walked through the front door, it was a powerful learning experience with a dramatic financial impact of a $4.1M shortfall to budget. Assumptions can't replace understanding your industry benchmarks. Now for all our schools we do 5 "touches" for each applicant during the summer months. We also know that we need 2.5 applications for every child we expect to show up to school on Day 1. Our solid enrollment numbers show what a difference understanding these important practices makes. Painful mistakes can be excellent teachers.

## Detours vs. Staying on Course

Let's say you've done the research, gotten the feedback, vetted your ideas, and finally written your polished, thoughtful business plan. You've got the people and capital in place. It's go time.

Now what? In almost every instance, from day one, things are not going to go precisely as you planned. How will you know when you need to make changes, whether big or small? How fast or how slowly should you move or pivot? Where is the roadmap for your entrepreneurial journey?

I've come to appreciate that the truly great businesses know their Key Performance Indicators (KPIs) so well that they are tracking them on no more than a one to two day basis. That's right. They know what has to happen literally *every day* in order to hit their long term goals. If this seems impossible to imagine, consider how most of us think about losing weight. If we set ourselves the goal to lose one pound a week and we want to lose 15 pounds, we do the math and mark the date on the calendar 15 weeks out. If at the end of week 1 we haven't lost any weight, we know next week we either have to lose 2 pounds or we won't make our target. We don't wait 15 weeks before we step on the scale. Makes sense, right?

But somehow too often entrepreneurs don't build this type of incremental approach into their management practices. They set very ambitious goals, immerse themselves in the day to day operations, then at year's end nervously review their performance – or their Progress Towards Goals (PTGs). At which point they either celebrate or commiserate.

Don't wait. There is a daily, weekly, monthly metric that can tell you whether you're on track or not. At the end of each day, week, month, quarter, half year, etc. you need to know where you are. Part of understanding your industry and managing your specific business is having the ability to identify the metrics that show if you are on or off track and, when necessary, taking corrective action quickly.

To my mind, entrepreneurs have a choice. Do you want to do regular wellness checks or an autopsy? An end of year analysis of your results is an autopsy. That year, and that opportunity to change your annual results, is dead and gone by the time you arrive at this point. It's way too late to be checking in on December 31st when there's nothing you can do to fix the results. For investors and your team, all you can do is celebrate the victories and try to come up with solutions for areas where you came up short. But if you commit to having regular checkups (daily or weekly at most), each review is an opportunity to course correct and keep you on the path to year end success.

Every industry has its own science of key performance measurement. Do you know what the KPIs are for your industry?

When we launched the Charles J. Ogletree, Jr. Scholarship Fund[7] while I was in law school, we made one-time scholarship awards and never formally monitored the annual progress of our scholars after they received their award. We didn't know about the KPIs for higher education. Back then we thought we could check in at the end of the

---

[7] Named for Harvard Law professor Charles J. Ogletree, Jr.

year to see how many students had made it. We know now that providing money is only one part of an impactful scholarship program.

While exploring ways to grow programming in one of our current organizations, KC Scholars, we spoke with college educators to discover what they already knew about KPIs for tracking academic success. Dr. Mun Y. Choi, President of the University of Missouri, told us his university knew on a monthly basis if students were on track or off track for graduation. The university monitors KPIs that have proven to be excellent predictors, things like attendance rates, quiz scores, and assignment completion data. Some academic deans even know on a biweekly basis if students are staying on track to graduate by checking to see if students have enough course credits, are taking the appropriate course load, and are leveraging relevant campus resources. Attention is also paid to some personal wellness indicators such as level of social engagement, participation in campus activities, friendships, and life outside the classroom.

We've applied the established science of academic KPIs to our KC Scholars program. In 2022 we awarded a record 775 college scholarships. Our goal is that at least 80% of those students will graduate on time. Understanding reliable KPIs helped us see that if we wait a full year or, worse yet, 4 or 5 years to see what happens, our scholars will not graduate at the rates that we want for them.

The founders of KC Scholars knew that providing a scholar with money directly may not help them as we anticipated because most colleges will deduct that scholarship amount from their potential award amount. With insights such as these, we have made changes to improve the efficacy of our program. First, it is much smarter to have a partnership with the institution. We pay them directly but as a "last dollar scholarship," meaning that the school must invest all that it would have had the scholar not received our scholarship. Second, if you provide a student with scholarship dollars but have no plan to follow up with them, how do you know how the student used the dollars? Did the money achieve its intended impact, or did family members influence them to help pay the rent or meet some other urgent need? Third, our scholars often need more than just financial support. Coaching and mentorship guidance enable scholars to have the confidence to choose the "right" fit school, the "right" major and receive guidance if they run into the inevitable challenges that emerge on a students' journey through college. Providing ongoing support also helps them navigate the unknowns of a college campus environment. Building a supportive community around the scholar while they are in college is equally important to the annual financial support they receive.

These insights prompted us to create a "wrap-around" approach for our KC Scholars program. Monitoring KPIs for each element of our program ensures that we maintain a 96% year over year retention of scholars and achieve our goal of 80% college graduation within 5 years for our scholars--figures that are more than three times the national average for first-generation, low-income students.

## Opportunity Outside the Plan

When the business model for KC Scholars was established by Jan Kraemer (Board Chair), Dr. Beth Tankersly (Founding CEO) and Aaron North (Kauffman Foundation) in 2016, it built on the 30-year history of Mr. Kauffman's Project Choice, later named Kauffman Scholars. When I became CEO of KC Scholars in 2022, I inherited a highly respected program with a solid track record. Our goal was to build on this solid foundation and to increase our impact, with the intention of helping 50,000 Kansas Citians by 2032.

I am very proud of the fact that in 2022 we awarded over $38M in college scholarships to young adults in Metro KC. On the one hand, that is an incredibly significant accomplishment; on the other, we knew that there were hundreds of qualified students that we were not able to support. Because we have to fundraise for every dollar of these scholarships, we are limited in the number we can award. In 2022, only 49% of our qualified applicants received scholarships. For many who did not receive our scholarship it meant that they would not be able to afford a college education.

We had to ask ourselves, "How do we help these other deserving scholars?" If we'd closed the door on new ideas outside of our established business model at this point, we would have effectively capped the impact the KC Scholars program could have.

Our leadership team kept returning to every aspect of our business model. Sitting around a conference table in meeting after meeting, our COO Natalie Lewis led us as we repeatedly asked some tough, fundamental questions, "Where can we find more financial resources? How much more can we generate through our own fundraising efforts? How are we going to grow to reach more deserving students?" The answer was not in our model. It was in revising and enlarging our model to include strategic partnerships.

We noticed in our conversations with university leadership that while many colleges and universities had increased their commitment to educating a more diverse student body, often they lacked the resources to recruit students of color and first generation scholars, and then set them on a firm path to ensure graduation.

Because we were willing to consider other ways to raise money beyond our own fundraising infrastructure, we realized we could approach universities who sincerely desired to serve the needs of diverse, high-quality students. If the university provided the funding, we could both find qualified students through our KC Scholars application process and then support them to high levels of success in college. We asked interested universities to make a multi-year, multi-million dollar commitment. UMKC was the first to sign on, committing $10M over 10 years. St. Mary's University was next, pledging $50M in scholarship funds over 10 years. Northwest Missouri State committed $17.25M over seven years. Several others made pledges as well. Although conversations with all of our university partners are still ongoing, we have already secured $90M additional dollars in additional scholarship funding with this new partnership model – nearly 2,000 additional students will now have the funding they need to go to college, graduate, and find family sustaining jobs that enable them to take care of themselves and their loved ones.

In addition, many colleges and universities award Pell grants, a federal subsidy for students with exceptional financial need who are pursuing their bachelor's degree. We discovered that some colleges were doing well attracting Pell eligible students, but their graduation rates for these students were poor. We initiated meetings with select universities to make them an offer of partnership: What if we bring our "wrap around" coaching program to your campus for all your Pell students? While these conversations are still in their early stages, it is another important example of exploring multiple opportunities through mutually beneficial partnerships to scale impact.

If we had stayed focused solely on the tactical execution of our business plan, we'd be stuck raising money by ourselves as the only way forward. By making space for strategic thinking and freeing ourselves from the constraints of our formal, written plan, we were able to find a new vision for growth. Rethinking our strategy has put us on a trajectory to increase our impact exponentially, potentially enabling the number of scholars we support to grow from 775 to 7,000, 10,000, or maybe even more deserving students.

## Iteration Within Your Organization

The power of taking the "regular wellness check in" vs. the year-end "autopsy" approach is apparent in our organizational management practices as well. Especially in start-up or early stage companies, just getting through the day, week, month or quarter can become the sole focus of the leadership and staff. Short-term thinking and patchwork solutions may get you through, but they can also severely limit your organization's ability to grow and thrive. If you are stuck in short term thinking without long term goals and benchmarks along the way, it's very difficult to know if are you making progress. As one of my mentors once shared with me, "You may be finding your way through the trees, but do you know if you are even in the right forest?"

What I've learned is the significance of balancing time devoted to strategy and tactics. If the leadership never asks the staff to step back and make space for both reflection and long term, strategic thinking, other promising new paths through the forest, even those leading to bigger, healthier, boundless new opportunities, are impossible to see. The pivot that could have given you a big leap forward isn't seen in the blur of daily survival and tactical problem solving.

On a practical level, here's what we do. You have to commit real time and real resources to make this work. With our leadership team, we have daily huddles- just quick check-ins that share one quarterly or annual goal, progress toward that goal, and our top priority to move that goal forward that day. One minute per person, with a little time at the end for some quick remarks on the previous day or key announcements. These are followed by weekly tactical sessions where we again review progress towards 1-2 goals, what is and isn't working, but most significantly what we need to do to remove the barriers to progress and chart a strong course ahead.

Senior leaders meet weekly one on one with their direct reports to review goals, align priorities and ensure the resources are available to succeed. It's also an opportunity for strong and honest relationship building, coaching, problem-solving, and celebrating. Monthly, we meet for a total of two hours to discuss 1-2 strategic topics. In the course of our year, we might significantly advance 12-24 big strategic "rocks." Quarterly, we hold one another accountable and support one another when we report out on our 5 SMART goals for the year, sharing progress and reflections on why some strategies may or may not be working. These are intended to help each person track their quarterly progress toward their goals and help us collectively reach our objectives. These quarterly sessions enable managers to get honest answers to important questions like "Are you on track? If you're falling behind, how do we course correct together? What's helping or holding you back? What do you need from me or from the team to remove the barriers you're facing?

After each person presents their thoughts, their teammates provide thoughtful, caring, honest feedback about what they have seen or feel could be done better. We ask each staff person to sit quietly and absorb the comments. Then we ask that they write down what they are going to do differently. We suggest limiting this list to 1 or 2 things that they are going to build into their goals plan. It's like a revised contract we all make with and for each other. As senior leaders we are now responsible to check back with each of our direct report's progress. We've found making these management or operating mechanisms part of our organizational DNA encourages reflection, revision, and honesty about progress. Getting out of the daily tactical enables us to look higher and farther. It's good for people and good for the organization.

## Put on Your Bifocals

Successful leaders need to have clear vision. Sometimes that means seeing two sides of the same coin and knowing how to communicate what you see in the right way to the right audience.

I've found leaders need to be *bifocal* in their planning and execution. When you're securing capital, for example, you want to emphasize what makes your enterprise different and successful. Fundraising is necessary to grow your organization, and to earn people's investment or donation you have to sell the very best within your enterprise. Part of that includes honesty about areas for improvement – but like in a job interview, when a candidate confides that their area for growth is that they work too hard, you mostly have to highlight strengths. You must be able to convince your audience with all your spirit that you are doing the best possible work, as evidenced by your strong, measurable outcomes and your potential for future impact.

At PLA schools, for example, we can confidently claim transformation. We create schools with a nurturing culture of love and genuine caring. When we take over existing struggling schools, their enrollment grows, on average, by 23%. Parents can feel the difference in our schools, and they trust us. In a relatively short period of time, we have already transformed 10 F-rated schools into A and B rated schools. We took a school that had the most incidents of violence and behavior issues *of any school in the state* and transformed it to a high performing school with the fewest behavioral incidents in its district. Many of our schools have had the highest academic state test score growth of any schools in their district. Citing specific successes like these is essential to making the positive impression that will raise the money you will need to create more successes.

Then there's the other side of the coin, internal assessment. While I can cite successes, I might question our staff on why some of our metrics are disappointing. To this day I can still hear my father's gentle encouragement, "*It's good, but there's room for improvement.*" To be honest I did not appreciate it when he'd say that, but I've come to understand how many of my wisest leadership decisions still come from listening to his voice (well, his and my mom's). There is always "room for improvement," in part because when you are on a mission as a social entrepreneur, there is always unmet need. You must always want to get better.

If, however, you go into your fundraising pitch thinking about disappointing metrics or the specific areas needing improvement, you will not get the money you need to improve. You can be critical internally, but never let that dampen the power of your story for external ears.

With each venture I have undertaken, everything I have learned from every other enterprise, mentor, advisor, supporter, and talented co-worker provides a starting point. I like to think that while each initiative is a success in many ways, as a growing leader, each subsequent venture shows improvement, refinement, and new ways of thinking while retaining a certain Phalen flavor.

From the Charles Ogletree Scholarship Fund to BELL to Summer Advantage to PLA to PLA University to Great Jobs KC, I've gone on an entrepreneurial journey to provide educational opportunity, support, and advancement to tens of thousands of deserving youth and adults. With the recent incredibly generous donation of $50M from the Ewing Marion Kauffman Foundation, PLA U and Great Jobs KC are poised to help an additional 50,000 adults move from underemployment and unemployment into family supporting jobs. Making plans and constantly reflecting on areas for improvement, and committing to get better as an organization, created this opportunity. The process of iteration adds value not just within an organization, but each time you as an entrepreneur and leader build a new venture or expand your existing venture. Experience is an incredible teacher when you remain open to learning.

Being truly bifocal is about looking backward for what can be built upon and repurposed while also looking ahead to what remains to be done. It is about being able to unapologetically highlight your strengths, while in the next moment being brutally honest about what needs to be improved. "Scholars First" is the number one core value in all of my ventures. Keeping your core values in view for me means everything I do, every new iteration and implementation, will always be in service of a long term vision based on a careful plan but not limited by it.

**Key Takeaways**

1. Don't just have a vision. Make a plan.

2. Commit to using informed input and experience to refine your plan "99 times."

3. Build in industry specific KPIs, then check on progress regularly and often.

4. Look for opportunities beyond your plan.

5. Strategic partnerships can help you scale.

6. Develop "bifocal" vision enabling you to effectively lead and represent your organization.

# Chapter 4
# REMEMBER THAT MONEY MATTERS

---

*"Money is a terrible master but an excellent servant." - P.T. Barnum*

When any aspiring entrepreneurs share their initial plans with me, I often find myself offering this advice. First, you need to figure out how much growth capital you need to launch. Next, you will need to develop a solid business model that indicates how you will sustain and grow your organization. And finally, no matter how well you plan and fundraise, you will always need to be both creative and savvy about managing your cash flow.

I know this is all easier said than done. I know that because I have lived it.

## Optimism Alone Won't Pay the Bills

In the early days at BELL, we were struggling to keep the lights on and make payroll. The concept behind our program was solid. We could see we were making a difference in children's lives, in part because of our commitment to operate at a 1-to-3 teacher to student ratio. There was considerable financial pressure to switch to the more conventional 1-to-8 ratio that would have simultaneously lowered our overhead and expanded the impact of our revenue. In my fervor to preserve our 1-to-3 model I thought the universe would provide---our students needed us, the program was effective, and this was work worth doing. Surely we could increase our fundraising and find more donors who shared our vision and would provide the support we needed.

Enthusiasm and firm convictions were not enough to find more money. Soon we'd reached the point where our bank account barely held enough for the bi-weekly payroll. With $30,000 in the bank and a $20,000 payroll I had to face the fact that we were essentially out of money.

Accounts payable were beginning to pile up. Accounts receivable weren't keeping pace.

Every Sunday I kept to my routine of going to my parents' home to enjoy having breakfast together. This time I went knowing there was a conversation I had to have. "I need your help," I told my dad. I laid out the tight financial situation BELL was in. It's important to recall that my father was a banker, so first he had to give me a short lecture about cash flow. He reminded me that "businesses don't run on optimism." I knew I was being optimistic, but I didn't think pessimism drove businesses either. Lecture over, I asked him for $15,000 with the promise that I would be able to pay it back within 30 days. That was optimism speaking. I had no idea how I was going to pay it back that quickly. I thought (hoped) that maybe something we had in the fundraising pipeline would come through by then.

A grant did come through, enough that we were able to pay down some bills. But not enough to repay my parents' loan. I asked them for an "interest free" extension and of course my parents agreed. We did this dance, teetering on the edge of insolvency, watching anxiously as BELL's bank account dipped into single digits after each payroll cycle. But as Tom Cruise states in Top Gun, "you never leave your wingman." I was not going to let our program quality deteriorate by abandoning our 1-to-3 ratio. I just kept believing that we'd find the resources we needed to do more than barely hang on.

Family stepped in again. My brother Jimmy and sister-in-law Rosemary loaned me the money to pay my parents back, so I exchanged one debt for another. All of us at BELL looked to cut and save everywhere we could. Some of the staff stopped taking salaries. My COO took out a second mortgage on his house to get us some operating capital. It was a massive amount of stress, living hand to mouth for two years. Eventually we were able to repay Jimmy and Rosemary.

Finally, a donor offered to give us a huge infusion of support, $2.5M, with one caveat. We had to be debt free. I had been forgoing a salary and had also advanced my own money to keep the organization afloat, making me BELL's biggest creditor. My decision wasn't easy, but it was clear. I forgave the $400,000 owed to me in exchange for $2.5 M and a solid runway for BELL. You might consider this an expensive lesson, but it is one I never regretted. It certainly taught me that trusting fate is not a reliable way to fund your business.

## Money in the Bank

Before we launched BELL, I hadn't had much experience with financial risk. Partly because it was my first venture and because I was so sure that we had a strong program, my tolerance for risk was high. Or maybe my extreme optimism masked the level of risk we were taking on. My own risk profile is considerably different these days because I've seen how draining constant financial stress is on both leaders and their organizations.

It's hard to make a rule about how much capital one should raise prior to launch because people have varying risk profiles. But what I've come to believe is that ideally a social entrepreneur should have at least 6 months of capital, the money that allows you to make the critical staff hires that will be revenue generating. Of course, having 12 months of operating capital puts you in an even better position. This should be actual money in hand, not "pledges" for future support.

Raising money prior to proof of concept is really difficult. Some people simply won't ever give a start-up any funding. They prefer to take a "wait and see" approach. Often they'll suggest you should talk with other leaders whose organizations seem similar to yours to find out what they are doing and how it is going. This isn't the outcome you're looking for when you're making the rounds for seed funding. Plan to keep in touch with them when you have real results to share but invest your time identifying the funders who are willing to take a chance on start-ups and on you. These are the investors to cultivate with care.

## Build for Stability and Growth

Even those funders who are willing to take a risk on new ventures look for what steps you have built into your business model and operating plan to mitigate risk. I think about several critical components for risk management when I put together a plan:

- Design for "lean" start-up and operation

- Establish meaningful metrics to track progress

- Have a system to monitor key metrics *daily* and make corrections to shortfalls

- Develop and live by a cash flow chart

- Invest in people

## Lean-In

Perhaps one benefit of the workplace disruptions resulting from the Covid-19 pandemic is greater acceptance of remote work and "virtual" workplaces. Especially in the social impact sector, high overhead for office space and workplace amenities impose a burden on the financials. If you can design your organization to be a low cost operation without sacrificing talent, operating excellence, and impact, by all means start there. It is easier to launch from a lean model than to have to revert to one when circumstances change.

Even before the pandemic, we were tested during the 2008 recession. Many philanthropic organizations suffered major downturns in their endowments and consequently were struggling to meet their existing funding commitments. Many were not inviting new proposals from nonprofits looking for grants. Our Summer Advantage program was still in its early days, and we couldn't afford to lose any financial support. What we could do was pivot to show our funders we were willing to do everything possible to make their dollars go further. We decided to end our search for office space. All of our employees were asked to work from home, using their own computers, internet service, and cell phone plans.

We started very lean. Funders noticed and appreciated our strategic responsiveness. Our low overhead model enabled us to offer programming at within 10% of what the school systems were already paying. Being financially competitive meant we were able to retain funder support and expand our reach at a crucial time.

Admittedly, working from home pre-pandemic was not a good fit for some of our staff and they did not last very long. At the same time, we were now able to hire talent from anywhere in the country, a significant advantage. When we began researching best educational practices for PLA, our widely dispersed workforce enabled us to uncover best practices across many geographic locations without incurring significant travel expense. Compiling the results from staff in a range of locations gave us more comprehensive knowledge at lower cost that we would otherwise have had. Even more significantly, we were able to assemble an absolutely incredible team.

## Measure and Move

As I touched on in Chapter 3, we operate an established system of regular meetings to track our steady advance toward short, mid, and long term goals. One powerful way to reassure funders, especially in your early days, is to make sure you have *daily* metrics that allow you to know whether your business model assumptions are going to be true. This is absolutely critical during those first 6-12 months of operation when all of your assumptions run headfirst into reality. If your financial supporters see that you have committed to this level of scrutiny, it shows you share their need to mitigate risk.

Key assumptions are going to vary by business, but I can offer some that we routinely watch. For tracking fundraising inputs, we look at the number of face to face meetings held, the number of proposals written, and the litmus test of these efforts---how many dollars did we bring in? Fundraising is always a numbers game and quantity of effort is essential. But so are results. We watch these activities on a day to day basis. We need to understand daily if revenue is being generated against the business model assumptions. If not, why not? And what can we do to get back on track?

In the initial 6-12 months of startup, when "all hands on deck" can seem to be a daily requirement, as the leader you need to avoid getting drowned in the programmatic demands or operational challenges of the day. If you've hired the right people they will manage the operation, freeing you to hold the larger vision of performing to expectations and adjusting the business model as needed. This is your main and most important responsibility. The one job no one else can do.

## Cash Flows in (Slowly) and Out (Fast)

It may sound elementary to develop a cash flow chart but often it is anything but simple. At KC Scholars, for example, we have 96 employees, and our payroll is both predictable and steady. The complication comes from our significant spring and fall payments for scholarships. These are big outlays of cash representing millions of dollars. We have to keep a close eye on our bank balance year round to be ready to meet these outlays. By contrast our Summer Advantage program has only 4 employees year round. But in March we need cash to purchase new curriculum, then in June and July when we run extensive trainings and hire hundreds of program staff our payroll grows.

Most businesses experience some level of seasonality. When you create your cash flow chart, understanding your seasonal fluctuations will enable you to match needs against revenues. The job is to ensure you have the cash on hand to align with the monthly outflow. This, too, is the leader's single point of responsibility. Even in our organization, where Eva Spilker is our incredible President and CFO, part of her role is to "remind" me on a regular basis how much money we need and when we need it. My job is to deliver according to the cash flow timetable.

One important practice is to review your cash needs consistently and avoid making the mistake of confusing **revenue** for **cash.** A grant promised for February 1 is not the same as having that amount of cash in the bank on February 1. Being dogged about collecting your receivables is critical. In the nonprofit sector we should take a lesson from for-profit businesses who are very proactive about converting revenue to cash on hand. Are you set up to take advantage of the most expeditious way to collect money pledged or owed? Are you using systems like ACH or other tools to make sure the money hits your account on time? Do you have in place—and enforce—stiff penalties for late payers? We have found adopting such practices encourages prompt payment and that in turn helps cashflow. If you adopt the fastest, easiest way to collect and track receivables and use stiff penalties to motivate customers to pay on time, you will be saving valuable staff time on collections while fostering a healthier, less stressful systems of inflow and outlay.

One other aspect of financial management that warrants discussion is discretionary spending. Opinions vary about how tightly or loosely the budget should be controlled by the top executive. I am no longer ambivalent about control. Just as I believe the leader has the singular responsibility for cash flow, I believe it is also solely the leader's job to manage spending.

On the advice of a savvy advisor, I made the mistake early on of giving our executive directors (ED) control of their budgets. At the time we had EDs in Washington, D.C., Boston, and New York City. My advisor believed that budgetary control was an effective way to empower EDs to "own" their operations. My concern was that managing multi-million dollar budgets required more sophisticated financial management skills than they had. Financial savvy wasn't one of the qualifications we hired for, and my reservations soon proved justified. Our DC leader locked us into a 10 year lease that cost us millions – we only had 3 employees in DC and had a short term service commitment. Financial mistakes like this were misjudgments and misunderstandings, not malfeasance. But they were the sort of mistakes no organization can afford to make.

Since then, we've learned as an organization that tight controls work best with our skill set and priorities. We elected not to give our functionary leaders control of their budgets. No department head is sitting on a $1M budget and taking a "use it or lose it" approach to spending. PLA operates on a $123M annual budget, but there are tight expense controls in place. There is a limit to authorized spending, depending on your position in the organization, and every expense goes through a dual approval process. Finally, there is a separation of responsibilities, meaning the person paying the bill is different than the person entering the bill into our system. With this process, if someone buys a $22 pizza, me and our CFO, Eva, know about it. By going through the discipline of submitting requests for discretionary spending our staff learn what is reasonable, acceptable, and justifiable. Over time this makes the approval process predictable, productive, and effective. But no system is invincible.

Even the best laid plans sometimes collapse. Systems break, mistakes are made, forces beyond your control such as a recession or a pandemic suddenly, severely disrupt your operation. Your first response may be panic. That's normal. My advice is to quickly manage your emotions. You're not going to do your best thinking if you are in panic mode. What I try to do is to *spend 1 minute on the problem and all the rest of the time on the solution.*

This is another instance of developing "bifocal" vision as a leader. You start with Plan A, but you always have a Plan B – my dad taught me that. For financial matters it's a math problem. What is our worst case scenario, namely what will we have to do if we can't raise the money we need? In general, labor is always the greatest expense, so your Plan B may start with downsizing, or right sizing. I advise doing this planning first because it is really painful. Put together the list of people you may have to release. When you scan the names of actual people and think about the impact losing their job will have on them, accepting that responsibility is traumatic .

The next thing you'll say is "I do NOT want to have to let (fill in the blank) go." You have extra motivation to go back to Plan A and start generating options to avoid catastrophe. You might find yourself asking, "what can we do to accelerate commitments we already have?" or "can we get an advance on some of next year's grant?" If you have a contract with monthly payments, can you ask for payments sooner? If you are writing new contracts, can you add in a clause for a 3 month down payment? These are ways to solve, not a revenue need but a *cash flow* need. Come up with pivots and creative solutions to keep the money flowing when you are running short for reasons beyond your control.

## Your Investment in People

A lean operating model with low overhead, clear benchmarks for tracking daily progress, a realistic cash flow monitoring system, and effective financial controls is important for attracting funding. But only if you invest in the right people. Even though labor is probably your greatest expense, I have learned not to skimp on talent. If you are conscientious in evaluating the qualifications of your candidates, you can be more aggressive with compensation.

As a case in point, there is a wide range of compensation for someone in a development position. You can choose to pay anywhere from $45k to $145k or more. What should influence your decision is not how much money you can save, but what are the specific goals for this position. The gap between what the lowest paid individual can be expected to raise and the target for the higher paid person could be the difference between generating $250k or $1M a year.

Hire for what you need. Be clear about your expectations. At any level of compensation, provide the objective metrics to measure performance -- – what are the 5 SMART goals you expect the new team member to achieve one year from now? In some circumstances you may want to offer performance-based compensation. This isn't an approach that every potential employee feels comfortable with, but if you are clear and strategic about the objectives while keeping the criteria simple it can be a mutually beneficial arrangement. Take, for example, how our organization incentivizes enrollment. For every 100 new students enrolled, the Enrollment Coordinators receive a $1,000 performance bonus. For 200 new students, a $2,000 one time performance bonus is awarded. And so on. Performance-based systems can help you stay lean and create win-win situations that allow you to pay for great performance, when they have been carefully designed to support your organizational goals.

No matter which approach you take—straight salary, bonus based, or performance driven—as a leader you always need to recognize that compensation is not a proxy for hiring the right talent or for maintaining oversight over the achievement of their goals. Every employee must be expected to demonstrate their contribution to the organization. In turn, if they are having the desired impact, they have every right to be fairly compensated.

## Some Thoughts on Funding Sources and Business Models

Unlike for profit businesses that generate their revenues through the direct sale of goods and services, social impact enterprises look to grants, contracts, and donations as primary revenue sources. Over the years we have gained experience with each of these and have come to appreciate the different role each can play. Diversity in revenue streams is worth pursuing but you have to recognize that every different source requires special handling.

We have had a great deal of success with foundation grants. Typically, foundation grants are very competitive and require grant writing expertise. You have to be able to make a clear and compelling case for funding, and often the first hurdle is gaining entrance to the network of philanthropic organizations. You have to figure out how to open that door, and once you've been invited in, you'll need to be able to build and steward a lasting relationship with the funders.

Unlike many state or federal programs, funders rarely place restrictions on your operating model. They enter into the relationship trusting that you are the expert in your industry and have the knowledge and ability to bring about the impact your proposal describes. While this is an advantage, there are also potential downsides to foundation funding.

As I mentioned about the 2008 recession, funders' assets do rise and fall, at times causing changes in their grant programs. Even more common than adjustments in response to the economy, though, are shifts that may occur over time in their programmatic focus. Where once they invested heavily in education, their priorities may evolve to concentrate on early childhood health, for instance. Funders expect their grant recipients to find additional, sustainable sources for revenue. They are not signing on to support you forever. They may even decide to discontinue their funding for a year or two, to see how you address the need to fare without them. If your business model is wholly dependent on foundation grants, you run the risk of finding that single revenue stream inconsistent and insufficient.

Individual donors and family offices have the greatest freedom with their resources. They generally require very limited paperwork and reporting. Compliance needs for private donors often takes the form of regular, personal communication. If you're diligent about keeping them updated, sharing successes, inviting them to special events, and finding ways to show how meaningful their contributions are, their commitment to your program is likely to endure.

However, this level of personal engagement can cost you a great deal of time if not well managed. Do you have a system in place that triggers birthday reminders or anniversary dates? How about invitations to special events? Regular touches, like periodic newsletters, that bring gratification to the donor? You have to have the time and talent to manage this group of donors. If done effectively you can cultivate individual giving. With research and careful management, small donors may become true believers who make significant investments in your work. These may take the form of endowments, bequests, and estate planning options, revenue sources unique to the private donor.

As you build your business model, be open to what you can learn from the for-profit sector. If you have a business model that reflects plausible, sustainable revenue streams, you're more likely to convince funders and private donors to make a one-time investment or even to commit to support over 1, 3, or even 5 years.

When we began laying out our business plan for Great Jobs KC, a program that finds and trains local talent to fill well-paying, open jobs in the region, we looked into what thriving companies with large numbers of employees do to find talent. We looked at how placement agencies operate, charging fees as high as 25% of an executive's salary. We found that employers are used to spending real money to acquire talent. They regularly pay for advertising, recruitment events, tabling at job fairs, event sponsorships—a host of activities that may or may not be effective.

We built our program to deliver an in-demand product: workers with specific skills for open positions with competitive pricing. Our value proposition to regional employers was that first we'll train in professional (soft) skills like readiness to work, and then we'll train these workers in the specific professional skills your company needs, such as commercial driver's license (CDL), EKG Technician, welder, etc. Borrowing from for profit placement firms, our proposal stated that when you hire our graduates you pay us a small initial placement fee, and after 3 months you pay us another more substantial fee for retention. That became our model for attracting employers as customers.

When we showed the model to funders, we were quick to explain we were starting at below market rates to attract our first customers. We can raise the price later but first we must demonstrate that we can deliver on our value proposition. We set a target to generate $1M from this "fee for service" model and provided projections with the number of placements we would need to make in order for revenues to grow to $2.5M. Having a sound, research based model elicited the response we hoped for from potential supporters. They looked at it and said, "that's believable."

## The Bottom Line of Bottom Lines

Several times now I've mentioned what we as social impact entrepreneurs can learn from the for profit sector. There is much we can adopt that will make our organizations more robust. But there will always be one fundamental, inescapable difference between leading a non-profit or a for profit enterprise: Running a non-profit is harder.

It's pointless to talk about money management without facing a hard truth. A for profit business has 1 bottom line. Nonprofits have 2 bottom lines. You have to bring in more than you spend, just like the for profits, but more significantly, through the process of running your organization, you are *changing the world*. Even though I stress the importance of being "bifocal," having 2 bottom line focal points, 2 standards of measurement for success is much, much harder than having one.

A social impact enterprise has to have satisfied customers, just as for profits do. But the notion of "customer" is complex and not entirely transparent for a non-profit. If we use a restaurant as an example of a for profit, the customer expectations are set---customers want great tasting food, delivered in a timely way, surrounded by a friendly, pleasant ambience all adding up to a positive experience. It's a pretty clear transaction.

In our sector as educators, our primary customer is also the source for our mantra, "Scholars First." The scholars we serve are our primary customers, but they are not the "paying" customer. The payers might be multiple--foundations, individual donors, corporate contracts, and the government. We are bound to satisfy our "primary" customers, the scholars and their families, while being equally beholden to our "secondary" customers whose needs and expectations also must be met. If these two customer segments want different things, there's tension there.

Especially in times of financial stress, it is hard to resist the temptation to "chase the money" by going outside of your core mission to fill a funder's related or unrelated objectives. Not all money is helpful. Not when it causes you to lose focus on your "primary" customers to satisfy an outlier need of your "paying" customer." Keep your eye on the funding sources whose goals closely align with yours. Know that you might have two "paying customers" and if you want to run the quality program you want, you have to find a way to satisfy both. Even when there are contradictory interests.

It's up to you as the leader to make sure you deliver on your value proposition to both, without compromising on the quality of the experience or the level of impact either group expects.

Which brings us to our next chapter, about operations, implementation, and how to deliver on your promise.

**Key Takeaways:**

1. Confidence and optimism are no substitutes for a sound financial plan. Before you launch invest in building a realistic business model for sustainable operation and future growth.

2. Minimize overhead from the beginning, but don't skimp on your investment in the right people who will drive your success.

3. Know exactly what 3-5 goals new team members, if hired, will achieve one year from now.

4. Understand your cashflow needs and establish management systems to ensure these are met, particularly methods to collect as fast as possible.

5. Take full responsibility for the financial health of your organization.

6. Be strategic about the sources of funding you pursue. Look first for mission alignment.

# Chapter 5
# Fix What is Broken

————————

*"It isn't the mountains ahead to climb that wear you out; it's the pebble in your shoe." -Muhammad Ali*

Along with a purpose, all entrepreneurs bring to their organizations ideas about how they should lead. These may not be conscious decisions you make or actions you take. It may be behaviors or thought patterns you've absorbed from other leaders in your life. There is much we can all learn from observing good (and bad) behaviors. What my experience has taught me though is to recognize that the specific needs of your customers, your organization, culture, staff, and supporters require you to question your assumptions about leadership and best practices. There is no one size fits all way to lead. There is no single standard playbook that lays out the best operational model. Don't get stuck managing by methods that don't deliver results.

This chapter offers examples of how the constant evaluation of our management methodology led us to adopt new mechanisms to improve our chances for success. By experimenting and measuring results of various approaches, we've adopted practices that promote clarity of goals, ownership of decisions, effective use of data, and ongoing accountability throughout the organization.

## Monday Morning QB

I'm from Boston, so it goes without saying, and I state this unapologetically, that I am a huge New England Patriots football fan.

Early on it became my weekend ritual to watch the Patriots' Sunday games while sketching out my agenda for the leadership team and our weekly staff meeting. I thought, as the senior executive, this was my job---

telling my direct reports what I expected of them, what needed to be done, and when it had to happen. Over time I began to realize that this top down approach was not having the results I wanted to see or that the organization deserved. The leadership team followed my lead, but as our organization grew it was important that each team leader take on more decision-making responsibility and accountability. I once heard the true measure of any leader is his/her ability to build up other leaders around him/her.

My command and control method did not allow space for my leaders to grow into the roles we needed to fill. And trying to make all the key decisions for the entire organization was burning me out. I kept watching the Patriots on Sundays, but I began looking for a better way to lead.

My team and I researched how top organizations structure their management practices. What we found time and time again was the importance of giving senior leaders the space to identify what they as active participants on the leadership team *actually* needed to accomplish their goals. Not just accepting what the CEO thought *they should need.* The leadership team's individual goals and their team goals should be the basis for discussion during every key meeting. When individual and team goals are clearly stated, embraced as important, and are mission aligned, holding leaders accountable to their objectives proved to be a much more effective way to coordinate efforts and keep us on track as an organization.

Our leadership team meetings took a dynamic shift after we tried this approach. Now each senior leadership meeting follows the same format and I'm no longer driving the agenda. Each of my leaders own their portion of the agenda—reporting out on their data, identifying and presenting what they need, managing all of the steps to get what they need from other team members and owning the results.

The team sets the agenda based on what they need to talk about with their peers to get things unstuck or move closer to success with a particular project. My job is to continuously assess our progress as a team and maintain a birds' eye view on our organization. As discussed above, every member of the team has 1 minute to report on two of their goals.

We then go around the table and ask everyone to state what tactical challenges they want to discuss. Usually these relate to one or more of the areas in which they are not currently achieving their goals. The team relies on one another for advice, resources, and buy in. I am there to help facilitate. The discussion focuses on *specifics* of how each leader is going to be able to reach their individual and team goals, along with the resources and time they need. We do this as a group, making a commitment publicly and working in unison to help each other succeed.

Learning how to lead through individual and shared accountability has been a journey for all of us. It is still something of a work in progress. Sometimes people try to "cheat" the system by saying, "I don't have anything to discuss." Subtly adding, "Can we end the meeting early? I have some pressing work I really need to do today." If this starts to happen I may step in to restore focus on the dashboard and the relevant progress, gaps, and solutions. We're looking for real impact from our group efforts. When we don't "cheat", when we stay on tactics and solutions, we all benefit from the collective brilliance of the team.

## Spend Your Time on Solutions

The other discipline we're trying to improve is time management. To maximize our most precious resource, time, we have a meeting timekeeper who asks how much time each participant needs to describe their problem and to engage the team in coming up with solutions. The timekeeper then sets the timer and holds everyone to their allocated minutes.

One aspect of the discipline we're trying to master is to *describe the problem* in 1 minute or less. A lot of us are very facile at explaining the problem. We can add levels of detail and elaborate on the specifics so thoroughly that three weeks later we're still talking *about* the problem. Succinctly summarizing a problem is a key management skill. It shows you've thought about it, refined it, and you know precisely what the problem is. In many instances this is the first critical step toward a solution.

*Effective leaders need to be able to devote 10% of their time to problem description and 90% of their time on the solutions.*

Shifting how you allocate your problem vs. solution time gives you a much greater level of power for problem solving. In most instances as a leader, you'll be asked to make decisions with imperfect information. Throwing your challenges at someone else's feet instead of accepting the challenge yourself erodes your leadership power. Taking responsibility to make the call and own your decisions is what advances your leadership skills. It matters how you achieve the results you're expected to deliver. How you get there defines your leadership profile and competency. As one of my mentors taught me, decision making is a muscle. If you don't use it, you lose it. But if you use it, it will get stronger and stronger.

## A Menu of Meetings

It goes without saying that there are never enough hours in the day, days in the week, or months in the year to allow us to accomplish everything we hope to do. Managing the time we have as effectively as possible is our best tool for facilitating productivity. We have found that by adhering to a schedule of differently designed meetings we can get the most impact for the time we invest.

Our "menu" of meetings includes:

- Daily huddles

- Weekly tacticals

- Weekly one-on-ones

- Monthly strategy sessions

- Quarterly step backs

- Annual planning retreats

It might be helpful to look more closely at the mechanics of the most granular example--the Daily huddle, a goal setting meeting as part of the annual budget process, and the structure of our Annual Planning Retreat, dedicated to creating a vision for the year ahead.

The Daily huddle requires you to have the discipline to answer one single question: "What is the most important thing I'm going to do today? The answer does not lie in generating a list of random activities. It has to start with where you are in relation to your chief goals and how what you do today will bring you closer to achieving them.

The legendary entrepreneur John D. Rockefeller once hired a consultant to share with him the most important factors contributing to success. Before he could offer an answer, Rockefeller asked the consultant what his fees were. As the story goes, the consultant asked to be paid "whatever amount you think my advice is worth." The consultant told Rockefeller that one practice was critical to every successful endeavor. In essence that practice is to *know your long term goals, your annual goals, and your quarterly goals, and decide daily, "What is the most important thing I can do today to advance my goals?" Once you define that action, start your day with that task and don't stop doing it until it is done.* Rockefeller took in that advice, reached for his checkbook, and wrote out a check for $25,000. In today's economy that equates to nearly half a million dollars for 15 minutes of advice.

Without keeping your eye on the goal, your days are too easily consumed by tasks that occupy you without advancing you. Still, this is a very elusive skill to master. Our folks will get to the huddle and say, "Today I'm working on [XYZ activity]." That's not what the 1 minute is supposed to be. What we're aiming for is much more direct and laser focused, as in this example.

*"I've got 5 goals for the year. Today, I'm centering on my goal to raise $4m this year. So far this quarter I've only raised $100k, just 10% of my quarterly goal. I am in the red. The most important thing I'm going to do today is research how to get to [ABC foundation] to support our work. Yesterday I said the most important thing was to submit a proposal to [LMN foundation]. I achieved that and I'm feeling very good about that prospect."*

I know it seems mundane to repeat it but it's really hard to get people to learn this. Honestly, I struggle to follow this model. But think of it as another muscle that needs exercising and coaching. Your job as a leader is to model this behavior---what's the most important thing **you** are going to do today—and to hold your senior leaders to the same standard of consistent goal-driven dedication.

## All Eyes on the Scoreboard

A reliance on clear goals keeps surfacing throughout this chapter but we haven't yet looked at where these goals come from. Our annual process starts in March, three months ahead of our fiscal year. We have come to rely on an excellent planning tool for building your internal business processes, the Balanced Scorecard, mentioned in Chapter 3. To learn more about this tool, search out some of the many detailed examples and explanations available on the internet. (such as https://www.investopedia.com/terms/b/balancedscorecard.asp).

Our goal setting is a team effort engaging all members of the senior leadership team. As an organization, our target is to have no more than 5 SMART (Specific, Measurable, Achievable, Relevant, Time-bound) goals under each of the Balanced Scorecard headings. Typically, as we brainstorm ideas we may end up with 19 or 20 goals for each Balanced Scorecard column---far more than we can tackle. Through discussion and debate we whittle that list down to 5 we can all agree upon and get behind for each of the four verticals – customer, finances, systems/process development, and growth and sustainability. Arriving at consensus is an important part of the process because it will take all of us working in unison and helping each other to hit our organizational goals. Once we have our goals it becomes clearer what activities will tie to each goal. The science behind linking activities to goals creates a vivid throughline demonstrating how *everyone's efforts at every level of the organization contribute to the overall success.*

Let's say, for instance, that one of the key goals for financial sustainability is to maintain 90 days' cash reserves. As a member of the enrollment team, you may think your work has no impact on generating financial reserves, but if you work backwards through the steps required to achieve this goal you'll see that it is all interconnected. If, for example, the enrollment goal is to place 22 scholars in each classroom and instead you place only 16, that represents 6 empty seats that will not bring state revenue with them. Every empty seat means the organization is short

$10k. So as an enrollment staff member your efforts are very directly tied to helping us reach our financial reserves goal.

Once we have our Balanced Scorecard plan, each team leader shares it with their departments. The intent is to clearly demonstrate the tremendous value of individual effort.

## Game Over- Annual Planning Retreats

If as an organization we only looked forward without reviewing the past, most likely we'd fail to grow and thrive. To avoid repeating mistakes and to learn from our successes, part of our annual planning process is a reflection on how we did against our goals or what we refer to as evaluating our Progress Toward Goals (PTG).

We look at our organizational goals, department goals, and individual goals. Each member of the leadership team is expected to reflect on their accomplishments and present their insights to the group. If your goal was to raise $4m or award 1,000 scholarships, and you hit 60% of the goal, what can you share about the elements that helped contribute to that outcome? What lessons can we learn? How do these insights inform what your plan should be for next year?

It's painful to stand in front of your colleagues and admit to missing 4 of 5 goals. But there may be a reason that comes out through genuine reflection if you speak honestly—an unexpected external disruption like Covid, or a sudden downturn in the economy. For another team member, perhaps 3 of their 5 goals are completed and are safely in the green zone, they're close on another that's in the yellow zone, while another goal has fallen far short and is in the red. As a team we celebrate why you succeeded. Your reflections have helped you understand how you're going to hit that red goal next time. This is the main takeaway. You're carrying forward your red goal/s into the coming year because you still have to get that done for the organization to thrive. And in some cases, it becomes clear that you will never hit your goals. Knowing that sooner than later is also critical to the organization's success. Your choice as the leader is not always easy—"do I coach this person, or do I need to replace them?"

This is an exercise in public accountability, but in most cases it is also a public celebration. It's crucial to the morale and commitment of your direct reports to recognize the wins and not just showcase the losses. It's not an exercise in shaming. Because everyone is presenting to their peers, there's certainly healthy pressure to succeed and a positive sense of competition. No one wants to come to two annual meetings to report they've missed most of their goals. Everyone on the team understands that if that happens, chances are that that team member will not be in their position much longer. But for those who are exceeding their goals, public acknowledgment is also key. We want the entire team to see what work ethic, strategy, tactics and teamwork led to this success.

As the leader it's up to you to make sure the experience stays positive and supportive for the entire team. The main message is about reinforcing the importance of the mission. There are people in our schools who urgently need what we do—we've got to deliver on our promise to them. This is what's at stake—we have an opportunity to help children, and in some cases families, break out of generational cycles of poverty. This is the reason we're all here. People need us.

To be credible, the leader must hold everyone, including himself or herself, to the discipline of relentlessly pursuing their organizational goals. Don't let the team lose focus. I do this even in my one on one meetings. Each team leader submits a form 24 hours in advance of our session stating their 5 goals, and indicating if they are in the green, yellow, or red zone toward completion. Here's my goal, here is where I stand, here's the most important thing---I hold them to that format on a daily basis. Part of my discipline and responsibility as CEO means that I can tell you what the chief goal is for every one of the functional managers and organizations that I lead. If I don't hit my chief goal, none of my reports can hit theirs.

It's the responsibility of the CEO to get the right people on the bus in the right seats, as noted author Jim Collins observed in his classic book, *Good to Great.*[8] Otherwise, the leader will end up making all the

---

[8] Good to Great: Why Some Companies Make the Leap While Others Don't by Jim Collins

decisions if they're not careful, setting the leadership team back to early days when one person, often the founder, was the only one creating the agenda. If leaders do not effectively communicate the interconnection of all organizational goals they forfeit an opportunity. Leaders must make clear how the cascading effect of missing goals negatively impacts the entire organization. And conversely, how achieving our shared goals lifts the entire organization. Without recognizing the implications of its interdependency, no organization and no leadership team can be successful.

It comes back to developing the discipline to exercising your management muscles. I've found if you do goal setting and progress assessment the wrong way it can hurt your organization just like exercising the wrong way can damage your muscles.

## Don't Watch the Ball. Look at the Target.

I started this chapter with football, but my early connection to sports came through basketball.

Like many kids, I learned to play basketball in my driveway. Boston, where I grew up, has harsh, snowy winters that cause asphalt driveways to buckle, heave, and crack. My driveway slanted way down and had a big drain four inches lower than the rest of the drive that was seriously cracked. Playing ball on my driveway meant keeping my head down to watch where the ball landed with each dribble. If I looked up and the ball hit a crack I was likely to lose control because the ball would shoot off in a random direction. I practiced a lot. I played on and was a tri-captain on my high school team. But I didn't have the right form.

When I went to college my coach, Gary Manchel, saw the problems right away. If you're always looking down you can't see the defense. If your shooting form is poor you're not really shooting, you're just throwing the ball at the backboard. Your eyes matter—where you're looking when you release the ball matters.

Coach Manchel gave me a program of drills and exercises that would improve my game. It was intense. 500 shots a day; dribbling drills for an hour; lifting weights to get stronger; a hundred daily pushups; and more.

Over the summer between my freshman and sophomore year, my mom watched me follow this grueling program. At the end of that summer, she told me she had never seen any of her eight children work so hard at anything to get better. In my sophomore season my scoring average went from 8.3 to 21.8 points per game. I was elected captain that season and again the following year. Fully embracing the coaching I received allowed me to become much more successful, a lesson I never forgot.

A big part of managing for success is smart practice and targeted improvement. Two examples come to mind. Mistakenly, as a young manager I often relied on sarcasm as a way to provide feedback. It was an unconscious habit, and I didn't know how damaging this approach was until an employee privately called me on it. My sarcastic comments, she said, made the review process uncomfortable, unpleasant, and unproductive. Her criticism shocked me into realizing I had to change my ways. Like any habit it was hard to break but beginning that same day I worked to eliminate sarcasm from my communication style.

Time management is another area in which coaching, and practice helped me to improve. One of my mentors noticed that I often started my day mired in email. Frequently I would read an email, then come back to it three or even four times before responding. "Earl", he told me, "at the start of every day ask yourself 'what is the one most important thing I must do today? What is the second most important thing?' Set your priorities and do not move on to the next project until the most important priority has been completed." Email doesn't deserve that much of your time. Read it once and make a decision. It has been an effort to adopt these behaviors and there are still days when I backslide into vacillating over emails or letting peripheral issues derail my daily priorities. Practice may not result in "perfect", but my time management skills took a giant leap forward as I got better at sticking to this plan.

When it comes to improving your leadership skills, you want to develop your own muscle memory by repeatedly making decisions, honestly evaluating the results, and making necessary adjustments. This is modeling the behavior you want throughout your organization. And as a coach for your leadership team, you need to collaborate with each of your direct reports on a program that encourages and allows them to develop their own leadership abilities. No one star player can bring home a team championship. It takes coaching, practice, and the coordinated efforts of everyone throughout your organization to beat the competition and achieve your great mission.

---

### Key Takeaways

1. Good leaders know there is not only one way to lead.

2. Creating space for your staff to engage and be accountable strengthens an organization.

3. Invest time in devising solutions, not in describing problems.

4. Provide planning tools and evaluation metrics that consistently clarify goals and expectations.

---

# Chapter 6
# TAKE CARE OF YOUR TEAM

———■———

*"Pleasure in the job puts perfection in the work." -Aristotle*

Great ideas do not come from products, services, processes, or practices. Only people can create great ideas. It's not up to the leader to be the only one with great ideas. But it is your responsibility to create an environment in which great ideas can happen.

Without great people your organization will never thrive. Placing the right people in the right roles and ensuring their long-term commitment will always help position your organization for success. Attracting and selecting such high performers is only a first step. How well you lead your organization comes down to recognizing that there are four interrelated aspects of managing people: fostering a healthy organizational culture, creating incentives and consequences, taking care of the team, and taking care of yourself. You can have the best product, plan, and business model, but if the culture is wrong, you will lose. As the business consultant Peter Drucker famously observed, "Culture eats strategy for breakfast." It comes back to making sure your "why" forms the core of your organization and that others are able to fulfill their "why" by collaborating with and supporting you.

## Culture Matters

Because humans are inherently social creatures, our personal interactions and connections help shape our behaviors. Think about how you feel when you are assigned to a work team. How relieved and excited you are when you genuinely like the other team members. How stressed and annoyed you are when that is not the case. How much more willing you are to go the extra distance for co-workers you respect and admire. How much easier it is to settle for "good enough" when you are not invested in the team effort.

It has long been recognized that people don't work for a company. That's an abstract concept. Most employees at any level in an organization work for their direct manager, the person who influences how the workplace feels every single workday. As leaders, it's imperative that we are conscious of how our behavior nurtures employee engagement or has the opposite effect of promoting detached indifference.

In my early days building BELL, I experienced the tremendous power of a workplace built on a culture of family. We were a small group of young adults lacking in many resources but rich in our commitment to our mission. Our work and personal lives were closely intertwined. Every single day we ate lunch together. We used the time to discuss whatever was going on in our world. Lunch time wasn't an informal staff meeting. It was a chance to catch up on the big and small details of each other's lives. If you couldn't join in for one of these lunch get-togethers you felt like you missed out on the fun. Every Friday we gathered at the Blarney Stone pub in Dorchester for wings and fries and a chance to unwind together. And when there was a big life event like a wedding, the entire leadership team was on hand to mark the joyous moment.

The strong bonds of friendship and connection forged by so much shared time made hard conversations easier because they came from a place of respect and caring. Our shared core values of putting children first, striving for continuous improvement, and exhibiting gratitude guided our actions and our interactions. We were there to help each other stay focused and reach our impact goals. When you work in a culture that holds a special place for every individual, there is no tension in work/life balance. Your work and your life complement and support each other. I'm confident our close knit culture contributed to the amazing growth and impact BELL achieved.

BELL was mostly shaped in the early days by young adults whose personal lives were perhaps less complicated or demanding. But another motivation was the belief that we were united in a fight for children who needed us. If we were going to be effective, we had to show up with everything we have. From humble beginnings we eventually grew this organization to $27.5 M, staffed by hundreds of employees across multiple communities. When you're on a mission, it sets your priorities.

Over time, and as the organizations I've managed have become larger and more complex, I've come to realize the importance of intentionally determining the type of company culture you want. It always has to be positive and affirming. It always has to express clear and consistent core values. But it can have a very different character, in part determined by the challenges its mission seeks to overcome.

While BELL was very much a family culture, KC Scholars is entrepreneurial. The leadership team at KC Scholars grew quickly from 27 to 96 people within 18 months, and while our work is focused on Kansas City, our team is located in a number of different states. Some are virtual, some are hybrid, and some come to the office regularly. To be honest we are still trying to formulate our culture after disruptions caused by rapid growth, the pandemic, and new opportunities and challenges for our organization. As the senior leader, I have to think through intentionally what I want the feel to be for the entire team. Now, when many of us are participating in a virtual workplace, being intentional is more important than ever. Some of my teams I only know from voice or video. It makes it more difficult but no less important to be conscious of how well your managers embody the organization's core values. How well they are behaving and managing in a way that is aligned with those values. We are constantly checking in not just on results but on the development and advancement of our competencies – how we get the work done.

Of course, providing feedback and supporting professional development sometimes means having to have uncomfortable conversations. You want your managers to develop certain competencies and yet you sometimes see behaviors emerging that are not aligned with the culture you want. Results can't be gained at any cost. In my experience 80% of leaders prefer not to say anything if someone violates the culture, as if only the outcomes matter. That's not how you create a healthy workplace.

Effective leaders will model the behaviors they want to see in their culture. And they will not shrink from reminding their managers what a healthy culture requires of them. Sometimes it's stepping in when emotions are running high, privately coaching by saying, "I know you're angry but that's not how we talk to each other." Or, perhaps counter-intuitively, it is encouraging conflict, not for the sake of argument but based on respect. Being able to disagree without being disagreeable. If members of your leadership team think a proposal is weak or misaligned but they don't say anything, it's a lost opportunity. If their tendency is to corral other managers in the parking lot later and tell them what a dumb idea it is, it's destructive. As the senior leader you need to model the appropriate behaviors and create the environment where others feel safe to engage in difficult and sometimes rocky conversations. Their acts of respectful disagreement might create conflict but will push our thinking as a group and prevent us from going left when we should go right.

## Feedback Matters

When I was a young manager, I lacked the maturity and experience to have hard or awkward conversations. If someone did something that disappointed me I was much more likely to talk to seven other people about it and never bring it up with the person themselves. Finally, someone who I was venting my frustration with asked, "Have you talked to the person you're complaining about?" Well, no. I hadn't. It was so much easier to complain, but so thoroughly ineffectual. Talking about your disappointment can help you refine your understanding of what went wrong, but I've learned not to wait too long before sitting down with the person you're upset with to discuss the issue directly. For the good of your relationship and for the overall organization, it's necessary to talk through how their actions made you feel and why you don't want to have to feel that way again.

This is one form of direct feedback, but there are others that are equally valuable. It's unfortunate that too often coaching causes employees discomfort. When done correctly, regularly, and equitably—and by that I mean not showing favoritism or exempting certain "high performers" from the same standards of management expectations—feedback and coaching should make you feel comforted, not concerned. Some people feel their job is in jeopardy when they're getting coached. But in a healthy organization the opposite is true. Having a manager or colleague coach you signals that they think you have great potential. They want you to succeed, and they are here to help.

In my management style, feedback is actually a strong indication that someone brings a lot of value to our work. My comments are meant to strengthen their efforts. If I'm not providing ongoing feedback to someone it's because I've decided the party is over. They don't have what it takes to succeed and will soon realize they're not a good fit for the company. One word of caution about reaching this conclusion prematurely: Be sure you've put your people in positions where they can succeed. Good people will fail if they have been miscast in the wrong role that doesn't match their specific skills.

We've talked earlier about a smart approach to hiring and this applies to advancement within the organization as well. Hiring someone into a job description that is filled with activities is far less effective and empowering than hiring people who are given clear benchmarks for what success looks like in their position. Providing a new hire with specific goals, for example growing enrollment by 10%, or retaining 85% of your staff, or reaching a 90% persistence rate in children, is giving them a gift of clarity. Using the operating mechanisms we described in the previous chapter enables you to let people know where they are on their journey to achievement. They can't get there unless you embrace your role as a coach and mentor by giving regular feedback and assistance.

Feedback and coaching is how you facilitate individuals attaining their stretch assignments—challenging your key leaders to go beyond the accepted numbers and shoot higher. At PLA, we aim for 10% annual growth on the state test in both math and English Language Arts compared to the norm of 3%. But after setting the bar high, ask your leadership team members, "what do you need to get there? From me and your peers?" Every time we help each other, our culture grows stronger, and we benefit as leaders and as members of a healthy work community.

I'm proud and grateful that so many members of my leadership team have been with me for many years. I suspect it's not because I'm the easiest person to work with. Instead, I believe we have a bond based on honest feedback. When you are clear about your goals and provide people with the resources they need, it's ok to have high expectations.

And it's ok to be disappointed or even annoyed when they don't hit their goals. Some business books encourage managers to have what they refer to as "courageous conversations" about performance disappointments. To me that's not courage, it's Management 101. You can't lead and you can't encourage professional development if you are unwilling to be honest with your staff, especially when they have fallen short of their potential. But be sure to be equally attentive to their successes. I mentioned earlier that about 80% of managers fail to directly address behavior that undermines company culture. But 80% fail to acknowledge exceptional, culture reinforcing performance, too.

Keep your focus on rewarding the behaviors you want to see in your managers. Praise and celebrate great achievements. Address and look for shared solutions for missed targets. Maintain a clear emphasis on the importance of measurable **results.**

There are so many small ways to let your people know you see them. When I started at BELL, every weekend I would hand write notes to a few people I thought were really rocking it. The short notes gave specific feedback for what they'd done that week, like staying those extra hours, or going the extra mile. The messages, while simple, were authentic. I would do 2 or 3 of these each week and leave the notes on their desks Monday morning. Years later it surprised me to hear from employees what a powerful motivator these notes were for them. As you build your culture, make sure whatever you choose to do is genuine. We all want to be noticed for the effort we make every day. We all want to be appreciated for our contributions, the things we do to move the organization closer to achieving its mission.

## Compensation Matters

Back at BELL, as an early stage nonprofit, we didn't have much money to fund our operations. It was almost like missionary work, much like my year working at the shelter. All of my leadership team could hardly survive on the meager salaries we were able to pay. In a way our own lack of financial resources brought us closer to the people we were trying to serve.

We were young and passionate about making a difference. I think we all believed we were so blessed just to be able to do every day what we were called on earth to do—educate children and be of meaningful service to our community. I had been raised to value a superior work ethic. My parents instilled in me the understanding that you can only be great at something if you work harder than the next person. My purpose in life is the work that I am doing. Even today, there may be football playing on TV in the background but I'm working over the weekend. This issue of work/life balance has never made much make sense to me. I have always viewed work as an important part of my life, not something separate. What's important is to find the right work for you.

I think about earlier Black advocates for change, like Harriet Tubman. Tubman was an American abolitionist and activist who courageously escaped from southern slavery. Then, despite the passage of the Fugitive Slave Act, she went on to lead more than 70 slaves to their freedom using her own ingenuity and the Underground Railroad. When Harriet reached safety I'm sure she didn't think, "I've earned a two week vacation." She was always preparing for the next battle.

My heroes are people like Harriet Tubman who never stopped fighting for their beliefs. However, as I have matured as a leader, I've come to realize that my calling and commitment are not equally shared by everyone. There are great people who want to work 40 or 50 hours a week and not a minute more. Maybe their most important thing is a responsibility to family or caring for someone who depends on them. I have had to learn how to honor what other people need to do in their effort to balance life beyond work. All of our lives are different, and I want to respect those who have their own way of achieving work /life balance. Love your family, dedicate yourself to worship, work out at your local gym, travel, pursue a hobby, do what keeps you healthy, happy, and sane. That goes for all employees and for all leaders as well.

Financial compensation also plays a role in creating a healthy work culture. I've come to realize that while our mission is very valuable to our staff, we need to be competitive with our compensation packages, too. In PLA's school districts we strive to be number 1, 2, or 3 in pay scale rankings. We build in performance rewards as cash bonuses. Every year except during Covid in 2020 we've awarded merit increases. We've expanded our bonus program, recognized more holidays, rewarded retention, as well as offered merit pay for achieving specific targets for academic growth and scholar retention. And we do all this while observing Henry Ford's standards of QQS---we judge merit based on the Quality of work, the Quantity of work, and the Spirit in which the work is carried out.

In my role as a board member for the Kauffman Foundation, I have learned a great deal from the manner in which Mr. Kauffman conducted his business. He created an innovative profit sharing program that created more millionaires in the Midwest than almost any other company ever has. While we can't replicate that approach in a nonprofit, his example prompted me to commit to more competitive pay scales and to develop performance based opportunities enabling those who are really rocking it to earn even more.

Money matters to people. It is necessary but not sufficient as a motivator. Competitive salaries and benefits won't compensate for a mission that doesn't excite and engage your people. Seeing how many families we are able to help gives great meaning and value to the work we do. Seeing our scholars progress brings all of us immense joy. Attending a graduation and seeing happy tears in the eyes of tough teenage boys who never thought they'd make it across the graduation line. Watching their proud parents who see how one child's success inspires their other children to do more. We all want to be paid fairly for the time we devote to work. But knowing our work matters to others is another form of compensation worth striving toward.

## Genuine Connection Matters

The pandemic caused major disruptions in every workplace. As we try to define a new normal, leaders have a serious challenge: How can you intentionally build culture when your staff have adopted hybrid or remote ways of working? Thinking back to my BELL days, I see how our culture grew strong from all the face to face, regular interactions and socializing we were able to enjoy. Without those informal, in person encounters, our ways of relating in the current "virtual" workplace can easily become simply transactional. We lack a human connection when all of our contacts are only about getting things done.

Even sharing information becomes more difficult over distances. Because information can be currency---there's a perceived value in knowing something others do not---we are trying to build a culture that is better at consistent communication. We try to cascade information to all our teams through multiple channels such as daily huddles, a biweekly newsletter, and town hall meetings twice a year. We also employ anonymous surveys to solicit insights into how our teams are feeling about the organization and their future. By creating an outflow and inflow of information we are trying to be systematic about enhancing communication company wide.

In the past I have been somewhat skeptical about the value of team building exercises. However, we recently asked our senior leadership team to participate in some culture building exercises that proved to be very revealing. It showed me that, when done well, taking time out of our hectic schedules to have shared experiences can contribute to fostering more human, less transactional work environments. I'm coming to see the value of being intentional about team building activities. They can show you why people work and act differently, and that understanding can lead to enhanced cooperation. Your culture learns to recognize and value these differences.

Our operating mechanisms need to evolve to fill the gaps in spontaneous culture creation now that we're remote. Leaders need to be intentional about setting up opportunities to connect us as humans. The days at BELL when we gathered for lunch are much more difficult in this new workplace. But rather than lose those relationships, can we find other ways to bridge the distance? I have begun considering sending out DoorDash gift cards and scheduling regular group lunches. Lunch over zoom may not be as much fun as wings and fries at the Blarney Stone, but it's a start.

**Key Takeaways**

Be intentional in your culture creation, making sure your culture aligns with your mission and values.

Leaders must model the behaviors they want to see throughout the organization.

Make honest feedback and constructive coaching a key element of your culture.

Recognize and respect everyone's need for equitable compensation and a healthy work/life balance, including your own.

Find ways to foster genuine personal connections even in a "virtual" workplace.

# Chapter 7
# Always Keep Faith

—■—

*"Whatever fear I have inside, my desire to win is always stronger." - Serena Williams*

I n this final chapter I'd like to speak frankly about two subjects that often go unmentioned in books about business and leadership: faith and anger. Despite the fact that they are often overlooked or undervalued, faith and anger have helped shape who I am, and they continue to both guide and motivate me.

We've discussed the need for leaders to be able to identify threats to the organization's goals and be prepared to deal with them courageously and quickly. We've explored the crucial importance of building an intentional, healthy organizational culture that values your employees and the people you serve. As you strive to do all of this to the best of your ability, there are going to be headwinds and setbacks. As the heavyweight champion boxer Mike Tyson memorably said, "Everyone has a plan, until they get punched in the mouth."

What has served me as a powerful way to face challenges head on is the ability to maintain belief in myself and in my "why". Self-belief will help you lead justly and consistently. But self-belief is only one part of genuine leadership. To enable your organization to fulfill its mission, you will also need faith. This type of faith is not limited by specific religious beliefs. It is a gift from family, friends, and the communities you serve. Throughout my career, the prayers, thoughts, donations, encouragement, and love people have so generously bestowed on me have sustained me through many tough times.

In addition to the positive power of faith, I have also learned to convert what could be the negative emotion of anger into a motivator. Anger can fuel your competitive drive and keep you laser focused on the urgency of your mission. Thinking back on my professional journey brings to mind examples how setbacks, course corrections, self-belief, faith, and anger are all part of evolving and maturing as a leader.

# Internal Problem, External Ally

For many of the organizations I have been part of in the past, I have been both CEO and board chairman. I may not have always held the title of board chair but in reality I was primarily the one performing key board chair functions: recruiting and onboarding new board members, setting the agenda for meetings, and generally proposing the issues for board involvement. An informal model such as this works when the board comprises friendly community members such as family, friends, professors, champions, community leaders, and familiar supporters. I have been blessed to have formed and worked with a number of somewhat informal boards such as these. But with organizational growth and complexity, boards lacking a more formal structure began to show their limitations.

Well intentioned board members began to invest their energy and attention less in governance and more in management and day to day operational issues. The warning sign flashed when a long time board member told me that she had heard from a parent who was disappointed with the service we were providing. The board member proposed that we all meet together to discuss the parent's complaints and decide what to do. It was uncomfortably apparent to me that the informality of the board structure was causing confusion. Allowing board members to get directly involved in operations and insert themselves into customer conflict resolution would spell disaster for my leadership team and our professional staff. We were asking our unpaid, volunteer board members to offer guidance and advice about the governance of the organization, not about how to do our jobs. She should have reported the complaint to me and my leadership team, allowed us to work with the parent to resolve the conflict and then report back to her on the resolution. She didn't want to do that. She, like many board members that I have experienced, either did not know the distinction between management and governance or did know the difference but would still prefer to step in to day to day management. Because of my loose structure, I was faced with a hard decision: how do you "fire" a volunteer and tell them their "help" is misdirected?

The lack of structure that enabled us to build friendly boards proved to be a liability. We did not have in place simple best practices like written job descriptions that were shared with and signed off on by every new board member; a training program for new board members; a set of clear expectations for what the board were to do and not to do - without those clear roles some well-intentioned board members drifted into proposing actions that perhaps felt to them more comfortable and useful. It was awkward at best to have to lay down new rules, beginning with explaining why no board member would ever be invited to a one-on-one meeting with a parent. That's absolutely not what a board member is supposed to do.

In this particular instance, volunteer board members had faithfully served for 6, 7, even as many as 9 years. We had no term limits and no process by which members could leave the board gracefully to make way for new participants. The current board members had not been chosen to fill specific skills that would improve our governing ability. By assembling a board based on friends and family and warm supporters, I had created an awkward situation that was difficult to remedy since there were so few processes in place. I wasn't sure how to proceed but I knew fundamental changes had to be made.

The solution we turned to involved hiring a professional consultant. We asked the consultant to do a board assessment, identify the weaknesses in our board processes, and recommend an implementation plan for adopting accepted best practices for the board composition and operation.

Our consultant helped us to develop key processes for the entry and exit of board members. We were able to design a matrix of desirable skills for board members to guide us in the recruitment and selection process. We saw the value of creating committees to go deeper in certain areas of board issues such as governance, finance/audit, and development. With the help of the consultant, we were able to offer long time board members a graceful exit if they chose to step down after giving many years of service. These were all changes it would have been painful to implement without the intervention of a professional third party. And even with that help we had to move slowly to avoid damaging important relationships. The process showed me the importance of assembling a mission aligned board in a thoughtful way from the outset.

Redefining our approach to board operations also pointed out the tradeoff a leader, especially a founder, makes by moving from an informal to a formal, standardized board environment. Under a more formal board structure I surrendered some of the control I had exercised as a founder or de facto board chair. The less formal boards were populated with people I considered friends. These board members came to the role out of a sense of duty and commitment to me personally. As we professionalized the board over time, these personal relationships gave way to new board members who were recruited for their specific skills, not by me but by other board members. That previous strength of personal relationship and loyalty was no longer in place. Trust and respect had to be built one person at a time. The danger, especially for founders, is that the board comes to view them simply as an employee of the board.

Having a professional board structure is something I now consider a must. But my advice to all leaders who are building boards is to put thoughtful work into how you will remain influential in the governance of your organization. Stay active in recruiting board members, dedicate time and energy to cultivating strong relationships with your board, do not let new board members come on lightly and keep all eyes focused on achieving the mission of your organization. Lean more towards tight versus loose control and maintain your self-belief and trust in your "why" to guide your decisions as you engage others in the governance of your organization.

## Faith Comes in Many Forms

When you think of faith, it's natural that church services and prayers spring to mind. I am constantly amazed and humbled by the sheer number of people who tell me they are praying for my success and praying that I continue to lead with passion. It's beyond amazing to know our work giving thousands of children and adults a fair chance in life finds its way into people's heartfelt prayers. Even when the prayerful don't quite know my name.

Some years ago one of my leadership team members brought me a message her mother had urged her to deliver. "Tell Carl I pray for him every day." That's not a typo. These many years later this devout woman still calls me "Carl". But I have faith that her prayers for me are heard nonetheless.

Faith to me includes prayer and religion but in its largest sense it is more than that. Faith is looking into an empty space and creating something others couldn't see or even pushed against and said couldn't be done. Faith is the ability to see the unseen and know it to be true, even when others claim it's the wrong thing to do or it's impossible. If you are an aspiring entrepreneur, how can you look at something that's never been done before and believe you can create and lead an organization to accomplish that very audacious thing? Your vision must be based on faith.

Our organizations are all tackling daunting, massive challenges. At Great Jobs KC, we believed we could raise an incredible amount of capital to start a workforce development program with the ambitious goal of helping 1,000 adults *a month* move from unemployment or underemployment to family and life sustaining jobs. Most believed that this was not possible.

When we started BELL very few organizations, fewer than 1 in 10, utilized out of school time to focus on tutoring. The naysayers told us "kids need to rest, they are over-stretched" and we should not build an academic program in some of the poorest communities in America around after school and summer hours. We took a different perspective, that of a parent whose child is in 8th grade but is only able to read at a 2nd or 3rd grade level – a parent whose child is functionally illiterate. Any parent in this situation wants help to enable their child to be successful. At the time, in the 1980-90s, using out of school hours for academics was seen as the wrong thing. We had faith that it was the right thing and we found parents who were more than willing to give it a try. And the children? For them it was a great experience. They didn't crave more down time. They wanted to learn.

Faith is why we refer to our students as "scholars." Despite their dismal scores and grades – all system failures, not a statement of our scholars' abilities – we believed the children we attracted to our program had more than enough intellectual genius to succeed on 3rd grade math tests if we were there to be part of their journey. Most people looked at these same kids and could not see that child as a genius. It takes faith to see beyond what the data seems to "prove."

Faith is an important part of who I am. I know my career has been successful because God or the Universe has moved in ways that have allowed me to succeed. Yes, I have done the work of relationship building, visioning, recruiting and retaining an extraordinary group of colleagues. My work ethic is high, and my advisors are exceptional. But to reach amazing milestones such as securing a $50M grant from the Kauffman Foundation (as part of a $186M performance based grant opportunity), God and the Universe are involved. That's part of my faith.

On the practical side, there are things every leader can do to build faith. I believe strongly in the power of visualization, and how it reinforces the impact of faith. I encourage leaders to write down the clearest vision or where they want to go and what they want to accomplish. Write it down simply but clearly and write it as if it has already occurred. Think of it as the TIME magazine article describing your legacy after your greatest aspirations have been achieved. Then sit with it.

As you reflect on your ambitions and goals, you'll begin to see and hear all the reasons you can't succeed. Many objections will arise – most coming from you. Political winds against you, inability to raise the capital, lack of expertise, the sheer difficulty of the job. Write down all of these objections on the same sheet of paper. Now challenge yourself to come up with the countermoves. How are you going to address each of these roadblocks? Until you can see the success in your mind complete with goals, obstacles, and solutions, faith alone won't make you successful. Your ability to close your eyes and see and fully celebrate what you will accomplish, despite not yet achieving your ambitions, is faith.

So far our Great Jobs KC program has helped thousands of adults enroll in training programs that will enable them to secure family sustaining jobs. Starting in November 2023, 1,000 adults per month will enter our program. With this scale and the success our students are achieving, many want to know how we are succeeding. We learned from others. Then we created our vision, tried to poke as many holes in it as we could, and set about eliminating the gaps. We were not deterred by those who pushed against our belief in what is possible. It's an ongoing process of learning and adjusting while never losing sight of our mission- to bring hope and achievement to thousands of adults struggling to create an economic future and a good life for themselves and their families.

Faith can show itself in big wins but also appears in more modest but moving ways. For many years I would get on a plane about 36 Sundays of the year and fly from Boston to Indianapolis to visit our new PLA schools. At the Indianapolis airport, John was always waiting behind the rental desk ready to help me. Each car rental was more than a transaction. John and I would take a few moments to stop and chat. Once he knew about my organization he'd also inquire about how the school year was going. We'd exchange news of our weekends, and generally got to know and like each other. John was retired but he'd taken on part-time work for National Rental Cars as a way to keep active. He liked interacting with customers as a way to keep his mind, body, and spirit active, and he enjoyed helping people. He was great, the absolute best at what he did. He was always kind to me, giving me upgrades when possible and making sure my rentals were ready to go. One Sunday evening when I arrived he said, "I have something for you next time you come through." That Thursday evening when I returned my rental car he handed me a personal check for $200 to support the work of our schools, PLA.

His was one of the most significant gifts I've ever received. John was an older Black gentleman who appreciated the work he saw me doing as a younger Black man. Although he was on a fixed income he wanted to contribute what he could to show his faith in the work we do for children. "I know this isn't much," he said, but he told me how much pride he felt when our program was featured on the TV news. I told him sincerely, "This is the greatest gift we have ever received." It's not about the money. It's the faith and the willingness people such as John have to do anything they can for us because of our mission.

# A Different Kind of Anger Management

The work leaders in social impact organizations do is so complex and so hard, whether it is managing personalities and balancing priorities, or trying to get that big grant, that experiencing some frustration and even anger is inevitable. The disappointment you feel when you discover you've got the wrong person in a key position. You thought you'd done everything necessary to set up a key leader for success, only to watch them falter. Consequently the impact you thought your team would make will be delayed by months. The disappointment you feel letting down the scholars and their families. It's an emotional churn. You feel blessed when you are able to help people but bitterly disappointed when you fall short.

Anger is even more powerful than frustration. As a young person I would often hold myself back from making my full effort, whether from fear of failure or an inability to fully commit. But when I found myself in a competitive situation, typically playing some sport with my brothers, I would get angry when I was losing, or when they would do something that upset me. Suddenly that flash of anger, not at them but at myself, triggered a response that made me let go of fear and a sense of my limitations. Instantly I began playing with 1,000% of my energy.

The Equal Justice Initiative (EJI) and its Legacy Museum in Montgomery, Alabama is a nearly overpowering reminder that for over 200 years white adults in United States have treated Black Americans in the most despicable ways. EJI does not shrink from depicting the pure evil that for centuries has been directed at my ancestors and relatives. Seeing pictures of men taking their young children to celebrate the castrations and lynchings of my ancestors makes me more than angry.

I use that anger in my work to move a B- grant proposal to an A+ grant winning effort. I channel that anger to enable me to have a hard conversation with an individual. That anger pushes me to understand history, and to recognize how little sacrifice I make to be in this blessed leadership position. Unlike Black activists before me, I face so few consequences for my actions. I am not teaching an enslaved person to read on a plantation where you could be killed for doing that. I am not exposing myself to the risk those brave individuals embraced by taking part in the Montgomery Bus Boycott, where I might lose my job by not getting on the bus. The Ku Klux Klan is not going to roll up in front of my home and terrorize my family with burning crosses or the threat of death. To resist injustice now does not carry the same risks our ancestors faced, but it is still not easy work. Successes are slow to come and often hard won. But seeing the current situations of inequality---how behaviors or conditions in one city (a murder, for instance) are allowed to persist when in the next more affluent town nearby they would never be tolerated as "unsolved", this is the entrenched form of social injustice we still have to battle.

My anger is not directed at other people. It is aimed toward the injustices I see around me. When I channel the anger inequality creates, it becomes a constructive force. Anger at injustice helps me to be a better, more committed, more impassioned leader. It unleashes that 1,000% energy that refuses to accept limitations.

Anger partnered with the inspiration that comes from seeing what is possible, what others have achieved, will build your resilience and determination. Recently I watched the 2007 film "Pride" about the PDR swim team ("Pride, Determination, Resilience" and a pun on Philadelphia Department of Recreation). When you see something like this film about a young Black man's efforts to use sports to teach the skills of teamwork and holding yourself to levels of excellence, it never fails to revive my belief that a more just society is possible. But more work is needed to bring about change.

In our social impact work the sources for inspiration are many. At a recent graduation ceremony for 105 James and Rosemary Phalen Leadership Academy high school seniors, an auditorium with seating for 500 people was overflowing, full of families beaming with joy. Proud parents watched their children earn a diploma, many against long odds. Younger children were seeing for the first time that academic success is possible for them too.

At a Great Jobs KC event, I had the opportunity to shake hands with a gentleman who recently completed the program. With tears in his eyes he recounted how he'd struggled for years, piecing together multiple low wage jobs with no benefits, barely able to support his family. After finishing our program he now had a CDL (commercial driver license) and was earning $85,000 a year with full benefits. Suddenly his future changed – for him and his family.

Within our own staff there is inspiring success too, as young team members grow into their careers. One such team was tasked to write a 300 page application to enable us to be approved for 10 charter schools in Indiana. They approached the job with tremendous uncertainty because none of them had ever done anything this hard. Imagine the joy and pride we all felt when their application succeeded. They had moved from believing "I can't do this" to the tremendous satisfaction of being able to say, "I did this."

Taken all together; our young scholars; our adults gaining genuine employment opportunities; our staff seeing what they can accomplish, these experiences inspire me to continue to push. So much of where we find meaning in work and life comes back to knowing your "why", believing in yourself, having and keeping faith with others, and letting your anger at the status quo propel you to action. Each of us can make a difference.

---

**Key Takeaways**

1. Prepare for even your best intentions and best laid plans to be met with resistance. Believing in your vision is essential.

2. Faith means seeing possibility where others do not.

3. Plan for deliberate actions to overcome obstacles.

4. Channel the emotion that will bring the best out of you and seek inspiration to provide motivation.

---

# In Closing

———————

Social entrepreneurship is the lifeblood of a healthy society. In America today, small enterprises are responsible for much of the job creation, and most innovations arise from risk takers who are willing to do what no one else has imagined possible.

If you've read this book, you may already have a strong "why" and a desire to take like-minded people with you on your mission to fill an urgent need. You need to trust that you can follow through on your vision, even when it feels as if you're the only believer. Keep taking that next step in faith.

As I began a career in social entrepreneurship, I was blessed to be surrounded by brilliant mentors and supported by smart, talented, dedicated colleagues. My family, friends, mentors and team members helped to push my expectations even further for what we could accomplish together. I still push myself hard. Ambitious people never lose the feeling of "*not enough*". Not enough time, not enough scale, not enough impact. I may never feel that I've done enough, but I know now that I *am* enough. And I want to spread that belief to all the people who fall outside our society's narrow view of an entrepreneur – women, people of color, people from underrepresented communities – anyone who doesn't get enough resources to address the most pressing, basic needs of our communities and society.

Trying to correct society's failings in a deeply unjust world can feel lonely and unattainable. It is difficult to be in the minority, having a vision that other people can't or won't see. Your job as a leader is to convince people that your vision, with their help, can be the new reality. As Dr. Martin Luther King Jr. famously said, "Almost always, the creative dedicated minority has made the world better." I want better for this next generation of Black and brown and female social entrepreneurs. I want to help create a world where there's nothing in their way.

The principles I leave you with are the ones we've explored in each chapter and that have proven so valuable to me.

1.  Commit to your "why."

2.  Find your people.

3.  Make a plan.

4.  Remember that money matters.

5.  Fix what is broken.

6.  Take care of your team.

7.  Always keep faith.

You will also need the courage it takes to act even in the face of tremendous fear. Courage partnered with persistence can make you unstoppable. There can be no failure if you stay true to your vision and continue to pursue your dreams. I hope you will find these principles useful wherever you are in your journey.

I look forward to the day we will learn from each other.

# About the Author

——■——

Earl Martin Phalen is one of K-12 education's most visionary leaders: a founder and CEO of multiple successful nonprofits, his mission is to deliver educational excellence and equity to low-income Black and brown children. Born into the Massachusetts foster care system, Earl was adopted into a large, loving Irish Catholic family at age two. His parents instilled the values that led him to a life of service, but growing up Black in a largely white, often hostile world made it hard for him to embrace his gifts. Earl's education taught him the power of Black self-determination, and the love of his family and community sustained him as he struggled to become the leader he'd once doubted he could be. Earl's exciting career is a testament to his mission's core message: all children deserve the support, the opportunity, and the self-belief they need to reach for their dreams without hesitation. He currently resides in Quincy, MA.